Understanding the Montessori Approach

This fully revised edition of *Understanding the Montessori Approach* is a much-needed source of information for those wishing to extend and consolidate their understanding of the Montessori approach and how it is used in the teaching and learning of young children. The book will enable the reader to analyse the essential elements of this approach to early childhood and its relationship to quality early years practice.

The second edition has been updated to reflect changes in the Early Years Foundation Stage and includes a fresh examination of the relationship between technology and the Montessori approach, as well as a brand new chapter, Learning in Montessori Settings. Exploring all areas of the curriculum including the organisation of Montessori schools, the environment, learning and teaching, and the outcomes for children, this book:

- examines the historical context of the Montessori approach and its relevance to modern-day education;
- explores Montessori's views of child development and the role of the learning environment in a child's educational development;
- details the organisation of Montessori schools worldwide and the structure of a typical day in a Montessori setting;
- highlights the principles of Montessori pedagogy, including the tools and strategies employed by its practitioners;
- considers how and what children learn in a Montessori setting and the links with EYFS 2017;
- includes new benefits and challenges of the Montessori approach to children's lives.

Understanding the Montessori Approach provides an accessible overview of this major pedagogical influence on early years practice, supported by case studies, examples, summaries and reflective practice questions. This new edition not only highlights the core ideas that practitioners should consider when reviewing and reflecting on their own practice, but also accomodates revisions to educational curriculum and policy in order to serve as an invaluable resource for students and practitioners alike.

Barbara Isaacs is Chief Education Officer, Montessori St. Nicholas Charity / Montessori Centre International.

Understanding the... Approach
Series Editors: Pat Brunton and Linda Thornton

This series provides a much-needed source of information for those wishing to extend and consolidate their understanding of international approaches to early years education and childcare. The books will enable the reader to analyse the essential elements of each approach and its relationship to quality early years practice.

Each book:

■ describes the key principles of the approach to early childhood with practical examples and case studies;
■ provides students and practitioners with the relevant information about a key pedagogical influence on high quality early years practice;
■ highlights the key ideas that practitioners should consider when reviewing and reflecting on their own practice;
■ can be used as the basis for continuing professional development and action research.

Written to support the work of all those in the field of early years education and childcare, these will be invaluable texts for students, early years and childcare practitioners, teachers, early years professionals, children's centre professionals, lecturers, advisory teachers, head teachers and setting managers.

Titles in this series:

Understanding the HighScope Approach   (978-0-415-58358-9)
Monica Wiltshire

Understanding the Te Whariki Approach   (978-0-415-61713-0)
Wendy Lee, Margaret Carr, Linda Mitchell and Brenda Soutar

Understanding the Steiner Waldorf Approach   (978-0-415-59716-6)
Janni Nicol and Jill Taplin

Understanding the Reggio Approach   (978-1-138-78438-3)
Linda Thornton and Pat Brunton

Understanding the Montessori Approach, 2nd edition (978-1-138-69053-0)
Barbara Isaacs

Understanding the Montessori Approach

Early Years Education in Practice

Second Edition

Barbara Isaacs

Routledge
Taylor & Francis Group

LONDON AND NEW YORK

Second edition published 2018
by Routledge
2 Park Square, Milton Park, Abingdon, Oxon, OX14 4RN

and by Routledge
711 Third Avenue, New York, NY 10017

Routledge is an imprint of the Taylor & Francis Group, an informa business

© 2018 Barbara Isaacs

The right of Barbara Isaacs to be identified as author of this work has been asserted by her in accordance with sections 77 and 78 of the Copyright, Designs and Patents Act 1988.

First edition published by Routledge 2012

British Library Cataloguing in Publication Data
A catalogue record for this book is available from the British Library

Library of Congress Cataloging in Publication Data
Names: Isaacs, Barbara, 1949- author.Title: Understanding the Montessori approach : early years education in practice / Barbara Isaacs.Description: Edition two. | New York : Routledge, 2018. | "First edition published by Routledge 2012"--T.p. verso. | Includes bibliographical references and index.
Identifiers: LCCN 2017038979 (print) | LCCN 2017039465 (ebook) | ISBN 9781315536880 (ebook) | ISBN 9781138690530 (Hardback) | ISBN 9781138690547 (Paperback) | ISBN 9781315536880 (Ebook)
Subjects: LCSH: Montessori method of education.
Classification: LCC LB1029.M75 (ebook) | LCC LB1029.M75 I85 2018 (print) | DDC 372.21--dc23LC record available at https://lccn.loc.gov/2017038979

ISBN: 978-1-138-69053-0 (hbk)
ISBN: 978-1-138-69054-7 (pbk)
ISBN: 978-1-315-53688-0 (ebk)

Typeset in Palatino
by Fish Books Ltd.

Dedication

This book is dedicated to Ffion Poppy Jenkins.

With her limitless possibilities she can well be the transformer of humanity, just as she is the creator. The child brings us great hope and a new vision.

(Montessori 2007a: 61)

Contents

Acknowledgements

I would like to thank the Routledge team, particularly Anna Marie Kino, for commissioning this book and for their support in making this book ready for publication.

My thanks go to my colleagues at Montessori Centre International who so generously, enthusiastically and tirelessly share their Montessori vision of the child and their knowledge and understanding of the Montessori approach with future generations of Montessori teachers.

I am also very grateful to my family for their patience and support in all my many Montessori adventures.

I would like to thank Happy Days Montessori School Wembley, and Montessori St. Nicholas, London for their kind permission to use the cover photograph.

Introduction

We do not see him ... as the helpless little creature lying with folded arms and outstretched body, in his weakness. We see the figure of the child who stands before us with his arms open, beckoning humanity to follow.

(Montessori 1992: 119)

Maria Montessori is one of the pioneers of early childhood education and has made a significant contribution to today's understanding of the principles of early years pedagogy. Her aim was to unfold the potential of each individual child. Her approach recognises that young children are active learners, needing choice and independence, whilst being guided by a sensitive teacher who facilitates their learning by preparing an environment favourable to their development. The children who benefit from these experiences grow into confident adults, keen to continue to learn and curious about life and all it has to offer, whilst being respectful and considerate. In Montessori's view, they are the heralds of social change.

This book offers a Montessori perspective in a series that focuses on specific approaches to early childhood education. Each volume highlights the ethos and values which underpin their unique pedagogy, yet they share strong links in the way the child is celebrated and honoured. Each one of the volumes within this series demonstrates the potential of early childhood education in transforming the lives of children.

Some of the titles relate to specific and recent curricula and approaches such as the New Zealand Te Whariki or the Forest Schools, whilst others have contributed to our understanding of early years care and education over a longer period of time beyond the early years, such as Steiner Waldorf and Montessori education. Like Steiner Waldorf's, Montessori's own view of education and pedagogy (Kramer 1976, Standing 1984) has been influenced by the work of Rousseau, Pestallozi, Itard and Sequin. In turn, her work had an impact on her 20th-century contemporaries such as Anna Freud, Susan Isaacs and the Macmillan sisters, who were also deeply engaged with children. We can also see traces of Montessori influence in the principles that underpin the Reggio approach. Their awareness of Montessori's writing enabled them to consider what she had to offer young children, reject or embrace her ideas and develop them further. It is in this spirit that Montessori teachers at Montessori Centre International are being educated in the Montessori approach – they are encouraged to be knowledgeable, reflective practitioners who let the child lead their ongoing learning.

There is no doubt that Montessori's writing continues to make contributions to our understanding of children in the 21st century. Her celebration and recognition of the young child as an active learner is embedded in current early years practice across the world. We also see her legacy in our understanding of the importance of the learning environments, as evidenced in the continuous provision advocated by the Early Years Foundation Stage (EYFS) (DfE 2017).

International aspects of Montessori education

Even before Montessori was able to establish the first Casa dei Bambini in the slums of Rome in 1907, she gained a reputation across Europe for her ideas about a child's need to learn through the senses as well as about woman's role in society. At the turn of the 20th century, she presented several papers at conferences in Berlin and London. Following the opening of the first Montessori nursery in the San Lorenzo district of Rome, she published her first book *The Montessori Method* (1964) in 1912, explaining her discoveries and views about young children's learning. In the summer of 1913 she conducted the first training course in Rome, which focused on her approach to teaching and learning of young children. All three events laid the foundation for Montessori teacher training and for the international interest in Montessori education, both of which continue to thrive today.

During the 2007 centenary of Montessori education, over 16,000 schools were indentified internationally as committed to the Montessori ethos and pedagogy, spanning from Sikkim in Asia to the Aboriginal communities of Australia, to South and North America, across Africa and into Europe. Montessori nurseries and schools operate primarily within the private sector. However, there are a growing number of state or government-run schools in the United States and Sweden, with continued support for

Montessori education in the Netherlands and an emerging interest in the United Kingdom.

In the UK there are approximately 800 Montessori schools, most of which provide Montessori education to children at the pre-school age. Many of these schools belong to the Montessori Schools Association (MSA), representing several thousand Montessori practitioners. Since 1995, when the funding of pre-school education was introduced across the UK, we have witnessed the growing professionalisation of the Montessori movement within the country. Montessori daycare and children's centres, nurseries and schools are demonstrating high standards in the delivery of Montessori education by meeting the statutory requirements of Ofsted, as well as participation in Montessori quality assurance schemes. However the introduction of 30 hours of free childcare for all three- and four-year-olds in England in September 2017 will bring many challenges to all nursery providers, including Montessori nurseries, particularly those offering sessional care. Nonetheless Montessori practice today continues to demonstrate the relevance and validity of the pedagogy – the root of the method's success lies in its focus on the individual child and the child's role in contributing to society.

Structure of the book

This book aims to take the reader on a journey – explaining the roots of the Montessori approach and its international impact, looking at how Montessori schools and classrooms are organised and how children from birth to the teenage years are supported in their learning. It also addresses some of the current challenges which Montessori education faces.

Chapter 1 explores the history of the Montessori approach and the reasons for its continued relevance and appeal in the 21st century. It examines the discoveries made by Montessori in the first Children's House and how they impact our practice, while also considering the global aspect of the Montessori approach and its significance to the lives of children today.

Chapter 2 examines Montessori's view of child development from birth to twelve and explains some of the specialist Montessori terms used in her writing. These are further elaborated upon in the glossary found in Appendix 2.

Chapter 3 focuses on the organisation of Montessori schools and the principles which underpin Montessori education across the various age groups. It presents examples of Montessori schools around the world and illustrates the structure of a typical day in a Montessori setting for babies and toddlers, nursery and primary-school-age children. Classroom organisation is explained alongside the changing role of the teacher as the child settles and grows older.

Chapter 4 examines the principles of child-centred learning across the age groups and the role of the teacher in facilitating learning in Montessori classrooms. The role of adults in supporting child-led care and education is discussed, as is the role of the key person and how this is implemented in Montessori settings. Observation as a key assessment tool is considered and the absence of formal testing discussed.

Chapter 5 explores what children are learning in Montessori classrooms across the age groups from babies to secondary school. It also examines how creativity and creative thinking are developed in the early years, explaining how the characteristics of effective learning are interpreted in Montessori nurseries and the challenges this may bring to some Montessori practices. The chapter closes with an examination of partnership with parents.

Chapter 6 explains the role of the learning environment as the key component facilitating children's learning and development in the Montessori approach, and some references are made to the EYFS (DfE 2017). An international perspective on the range of Montessori learning environments indicates the changes in the learning environment reflecting children's ages. The range of Montessori learning materials and activities is discussed in relation to children's stages of development and their learning environments. The role of the teacher in the context of preparation and maintenance of the environment is discussed.

Chapter 7 finally reflects on the benefits of self-directed learning and the contribution it makes to children's self-image in the context of criticism levied against the Montessori pedagogy. It also makes links with current research and Montessori's own vision for the future of humankind. It explores challenges to the Montessori approach presented by today's outcomes-led view of education.

The Appendices are intended to provide a resource for those wanting to find out more about Montessori education. They includes information about learning in Montessori secondary schools, a glossary of terms, a brief summary of key Montessori texts and a list of leading UK and international Montessori organisations.

The structure of chapters

Each chapter comprises a brief introduction summarising the content. It includes a discussion of the topic supported by relevant references to Montessori texts and to current research, as well as a critique of the Montessori approach where appropriate. The key points which appear at the end of each chapter are intended to highlight areas of interest for readers' consideration and to prompt reflections on the Montessori approach. It is hoped that the reflection included at the end of each chapter will engage readers in discussions with colleagues and fellow students regarding the significance of the Montessori method to their own practice. The references are intended to spark interest in further reading.

References

DfE (Department for Education) (2017) *Statutory Framework for Early Years Foundation Stage.* Online: www.gov.uk/government/uploads/system/uploads/attachment_data/file/596629/EYFS_STATUTORY_FRAMEWORK_2017.pdf

Kramer, R. (1976) *Maria Montessori.* London: Montessori International Publishing.

Montessori, M. (1964) [1912] *The Montessori Method.* New York: Schocken Books.

Montessori, M. (1992) [1949] *Education and Peace.* Oxford: ABC – Clio Ltd, Volume 10.

Standing, E.M. (1984) *Maria Montessori, Her Life and Work.* New York: Plume.

1 Historical context

This chapter explores the history of the Montessori approach and the reasons for its continued relevance and appeal in the 21st century. It also considers the global aspects of the Montessori approach and its bearing on the lives of children today. It examines the discoveries made by Montessori in the first Children's House and how those findings impact Montessori practice today.

> Education must concern itself with the development of individuality and allow the individual child to remain independent not only in the earliest years of childhood but through all the stages of his development. Two things are necessary: the development of individuality and the participation of the individual in a truly social life. This development and this participation in social activities will take different forms in the various stages of childhood. But one principle will remain unchanged during all these stages: the child must be furnished at all times with the means necessary for him to act and gain experience. His life as a social being will then develop throughout his formative years, becoming more and more complex as he grows older.
>
> (Montessori 1992: 56)

Montessori's beginnings

Montessori's early life

Montessori was born in Chiaravale, Ancona province, on the east coast of Italy on 31 August 1870, the year in which Italy became a republic. The new political structure heralded changes in society and spawned new possibilities for education. Montessori was one of the beneficiaries of the emerging new political and social trends in Italian society in the last three decades of the 19th century.

Montessori was the only child of Renilde Stoppani, a niece of the renowned naturalist Antonio Stoppani. Renilde supported her daughter's aspiration to study mathematics, the sciences and later, to become a doctor. Montessori's father, Alessandro, was of a military background and rather conservative in his outlook on life. As a civil servant he and his family moved several times until they finally settled in Rome in 1875, when Maria was five years old. At the age of fourteen the young Maria joined a technical school for boys, hoping to become an engineer. Her subsequent interest in biology led her towards the medical sciences. Gaining entry into the University of Rome to study medicine was a real challenge; she was opposed both by her father and the establishment. Nonetheless, she achieved her goal and entered the University of Rome School of Medicine in 1892.

Becoming a doctor

Her student life was not easy; she funded her university studies by tutoring and scholarships. As the only woman admitted into the programme of study, she faced ridicule and difficulties in attending some of the courses. For example, she was not able to participate in the dissection lectures because it was considered inappropriate for a woman to share the lessons with men. She had to work alone in the evenings. Kramer (1976) mentions that Montessori hated the smell of the dead bodies. This must have added a further obstacle and confirms her determination to become a doctor.

Montessori achieved her aim in 1896 when she graduated with double honours. For the first time her father acknowledged and applauded her determination to join the medical vocation. She was one of the first two women to become a doctor in Italy at the time. For the next ten years she devoted herself to practising medicine both in a small private clinic and in the hospitals of Rome, working with women and children. Her appointment as an assistant doctor at the Psychiatric Clinic of the University of Rome gave her the opportunity to gain a deeper insight into the lives of children with various levels of mental disability. They became her inspiration for further study and she focused on the work of two French doctors, Jean Itard (1775–1838) and Eduard Seguin (1812–1880). Following her study and observations of children in the Psychiatric Clinic, she formed the opinion that they needed suitable education more than medical treatment. She expressed this view for the first time at a meeting of teachers and lecturers in Turin in 1898. This was the beginning of Montessori's focus on pedagogy rather than medicine.

Following the Turin presentation, she was invited to give a series of lectures on the observation and training of children with disabilities to teachers in Rome. These lectures were instrumental in the foundation of the first state Orthophrenic School in the city. This meant that all the children with special needs in the city had the opportunity to attend. Montessori was the first director of this clinic. For the next two years she and her colleagues worked tirelessly to observe children and train teachers, testing and developing Sequin's and Itard's ideas in the process. Their efforts were recognised when some of the children from the Orthophrenic School passed state school examinations and were able to enter mainstream schools. This was the beginning of Montessori's consideration of general education for all children in Italy.

Medical profession leads Montessori towards work with children

At the same time, Montessori continued her advocacy on behalf of women and children. Her concerns for their plight were voiced at a feminist conference held in London in 1900, where she was critical of child labour and supported Queen Victoria's programme against it. Montessori's commitment to the rights of women and children continued until her death in 1952.

Some time between 1898 and 1900 Montessori gave birth to a son, Mario. We know that he was the son of Doctor Montessano, a medical colleague, whose aristocratic background barred marriage to Maria Montessori. However, there is a lack of clarity in the Montessori records as to when exactly Mario was born and why he was not given his father's name. He was brought up in the countryside outside Rome and Montessori visited him frequently. She revealed the truth about his parentage when he was fifteen; from then on Mario lived alongside his mother and became her assistant. Montessori never spoke about Mario's origins – he was known as her adopted son. Only at Mario's own funeral in 1982 was his father publically acknowledged for the first time. The 20th century gave us the opportunity to delve deeper in our understanding of the human psyche, and there is no doubt that Montessori's denial of her son during his early years must have had a profound effect both on her attitudes to children as well as her research and writing. We can only speculate on how her life would have unfolded had she kept Mario and brought him up herself.

Establishing the first Montessori nursery – the Casa dei Bambini in Rome

Following her work with teachers in Rome, Montessori realised that further study of the philosophy and anthropology of education would be beneficial to her, and she enrolled, once again, as a student at the University of Rome. It was during this time that Montessori translated the works of Itard and Sequin into Italian. In 1904 she became a Professor of Anthropology at the university. The ten years between her graduation in 1896 and 1906 can be seen as the preparatory period for the work which commenced in 1906. In that year Montessori was invited to set up a school in a newly built social housing estate in the San Lorenzo slum district of Rome, where migrants from the countryside and abroad came to live in search of work in the city. At that time in Italy, compulsory education started at the age of six, as it does today. The director of the housing project wanted children under that age to be looked after whilst their mothers went to work. Montessori was approached to lead this project and so began to establish the first Children's House (Casa dei Bambini). All she was given were the rooms for the nursery school. There was no money for furnishings, educational materials or teachers. Montessori had to be enormously resourceful in ensuring that her project succeeded.

Her team reassembled office furniture to make chairs and tables appropriate for a child's size. They introduced a range of toys donated to the school and also incorporated some of the materials Montessori trialled in the Orthophrenic School. There was no money to pay a teacher's salary, so Montessori employed the daughter of the caretaker to help her care for the children. When the school opened on 6 January 1907 at 53 Via Marsi, Montessori made a now famous speech in which she committed to provide well for the fifty children in her care (Montessori 2007b).

She began her project by ensuring that all the children attending were clean, weighed, measured and provided with nourishing food, so caring for their physical needs. She realised that the parents were keen to be involved and that the children had the power of introducing basic hygiene and orderly habits to their families. This was as much a social experiment as a pedagogical one. During the inaugural address delivered at the opening of the second Children's House in 1907 Montessori stated that traditionally:

> The home is shut off not only from education but also from social influences. In the Children's Houses we see for the first time the possibility of effectively establishing 'closer links.' This school is located in the same building as the children's homes and the teacher lives in the midst. The parents know the Children's House belongs to them ... They can go there at any hour of the day to watch, to admire, to meditate.
>
> (Montessori 2007b: 336)

Thus the school was placed at the heart of the community. This principle was mirrored by the parents who first established the Reggio Emilia nurseries after World War II (Edwards et al. 1998). Key too was how the schools looked to establish closer links between the children, their families and the whole community.

Montessori did not have preconceived ideas about the educational content of the programme she offered in the nursery. Rather, she observed the children and these observations constituted the basis of what we know today as the Montessori approach.

Observation remains at the heart of Montessori practice today and guides the educators' understanding of children in their care, and serves as the basis for their planning and assessment of children's progress.

The early days of Montessori education

Montessori's two-year engagement with the two Children's Houses in San Lorenzo and the establishment of the Casa dei Bambini in Milan's Umanitaria, a Jewish Socialist Centre, by Anna Maccheroni in 1908, contributed to discoveries documented by Montessori herself in *The Montessori Method* (1964 [1912]) and further elaborated upon by Kramer (1976), Standing (1984) and others.

Montessori's aim was to nurture each individual child so that she or he could reach her or his potential as a human being. She believed that this was made possible by providing a favourable environment which would nurture self-development under the guidance of sensitive and empathetic adults (MCI 2010). To achieve this aim, she instinctively recognised that movement and manipulation are the keys to learning in the early years and therefore that young children must be given opportunities to be 'active learners' (DfE 2017). This discovery translated into encouraging children to help look after the classroom and its environs, and to the development of materials for educating the senses. To this day, these two areas are the bedrock of all learning in Montessori nurseries.

Montessori (2007b) recognised that for unique development of each individual to take place, children needed freedom within limits to explore the favourable environment specially prepared to meet their developmental as well as individual needs. In an atmosphere of autonomy which is supplemented by a wide range of accessible activities, the child would reveal the true potential of the human being and should be nurtured to achieve it. She observed that children as young as three were able to select activities which engaged them and so were able to repeat them whilst deeply focusing on the task. This type of activity fulfilled the children's individual needs, demonstrated their ability to concentrate for long periods of time and facilitated development of self-discipline and awareness of others. This, for Montessori (2007a, 2007b), was the sign of true liberty. In the 1946 lectures (Montessori 2012: 133) she declared: 'if they [the children] don't become independent they can do nothing in the world'.

The children in the first Children's Houses demonstrated real satisfaction from the activities on offer. Montessori believed that the personal fulfilment gained from engaging in a self-chosen activity was a reward in itself; therefore there was no need for further praise. The spontaneous nature of children's learning also means that children who are able to become involved in activities embark on purposeful tasks and achieve satisfaction for their whole being without extrinsic incentives. Therefore, under these circumstances there is no need to establish rewards as a means of motivation or implement sanctions as a form of punishment. This idea, which underpins the Montessori approach, has been the cause of much misunderstanding and thus will be revisited in later chapters.

Even though Montessori initially employed the caretaker's daughter to help in the first Casa dei Bambini, she came to realise that if her findings from the first Children's House and her understanding of children were to be available to children outside the San Lorenzo district, she needed to share her research. Such was the interest in her work that she was able to offer the first training course for teachers in August 1909. This training course was followed by the publication of her first book *Il Metodo della Pedagogia Scientifica applicata all educazione infantile melle Casa dei Bambini*. The English translation was published under the title *The Montessori Method*. Montessori disliked this title because it implied that it was *her method* rather than the scientific pedagogy of observing children.

Her discoveries between 1907 and 1908 attracted much attention in the Italian and international press. This was possible because of printing innovations and the growth of cheap newsprint as well as general interest in education across the world, particularly in Europe and the US. Following the success of the first training course, which was attended by participants not only from Europe but also North America, South America and Asia, preparations were made to establish schools in all four continents. This coincided with the publication of articles about Montessori's work with children in US-based *McClure's Magazine* in May and December 1911. The publicity and interest in Montessori's first book contributed towards the decision to devote her time to teacher training and writing.

Montessori education around the world

Following the death of her mother in 1912, with whom she lived, the forty-two-year-old Montessori began to travel and deliver lectures not only in Italy but also abroad.

She offered the first international course in Rome in 1913 and it was attended by ninety students from all over the world. This was followed by a short visit to the US in December of the same year, where she met, amongst others, Alexander Graham Bell, Helen Keller and John Dewey. She also visited Harvard University. The Montessori Educational Association of America was established during her first visit. In 1914 a second international course was delivered in Rome, during which Anna Maccheroni, Montessori's friend and colleague who set up a school in Milan in 1908, participated in demonstration classes, while Claude Claremont, engineer and fellow of the British Psychological Society, acted as an interpreter. The following year Montessori returned to the US to participate in the San Francisco Pan American Exhibition, where she established a Montessori classroom in a specially constructed glass pavilion so that visitors could witness the Montessori classroom in action. This was also the first time Mario accompanied his mother on an international visit.

However, Montessori was never to return to the US. This was the result of criticism of her work by William H. Kilpatrick (1914), an influential pedagogue of the day. It is thanks to the efforts of Nancy McCormick Rambusch that awareness of the Montessori approach was revived in North America in the 1950s. Rambusch was also the first president of the American Montessori Society (AMS), which has become one of the leading organisations in Montessori education in the US today. The influence of the AMS is growing internationally.

Montessori spent much of her time between the two world wars in Europe working first in Spain and then in England. At this time she developed ideas for the education of primary-school-age children, which were published around 1917 in two volumes entitled *The Advanced Montessori Method* (1991, 2007f). In 1920 Montessori visited Amsterdam for the first time, and there she found a country ready to embrace her ideas. *The Call to Education*, a magazine edited by Montessori and published in Amsterdam in 1924 and 1925, documented the growth of the Montessori movement in countries as far apart as Panama, South Africa and Bulgaria. To this day the Netherlands is the only country in the world where Montessori schools operate as an integral part of the education system and are funded by the state from the age of three to eleven, giving parents a true choice in their children's early education. Montessori training is offered as postgraduate study for Dutch qualified teachers.

The period between the two world wars was very productive for Montessori, with the establishment of Association Montessori Internationale in Amsterdam in 1926 followed by a seminal lecture to the League of Nations on 'Education and Peace' in the same year. In 1929 she published *The Montessori Method* in a new edition. Addressing her displeasure at the original title in English, she renamed it *The Discovery of the Child* (2007b). It is interesting to note the differences in the two versions of the book, documenting Montessori's reflection on her own practice and changing views in the twenty years since its first edition. The foreword of the second edition identifies the existence of Montessori schools across the world from Japan to Morocco, Egypt to New Zealand, Canada to Russia, Syria to Java. It also acknowledges translation of the book into fourteen languages including Arabic, Japanese, Chinese and Gujarati, as well as many European languages.

Montessori witnessed the outbreak of the Spanish Civil War in Barcelona and was in India when World War II broke out. She was joined in India by Mario and remained there until 1946. Upon her return to Europe she settled in the Netherlands, near her son and his family. She was active in supporting the establishment of United Nations Educational, Scientific and Cultural Organisation (UNESCO) by becoming one of its founding members. She was nominated for the Nobel Peace Prize for her efforts towards international peace. She felt passionately that the future of harmonious co-existence on the planet lay in the hands of the child. She continued to lecture until the year of her death. She was preparing for a trip to Ghana when she died in May 1952. She is buried in Noordwijk-on-Sea, the Netherlands. Her grave indicates that she wanted to be remembered as a 'Citizen of the World'. The BBC archive has an interview with Mario following her death. He recollects his mother as someone who loved cooking and who enjoyed spending time with her four grand-children.

During celebrations of the 100th anniversary of the establishment of the first Casa dei Bambini, Montessori organisations conducted an international survey of Montessori schools. It identified 22,000 schools in over 100 countries of the world, a powerful testimonial to the relevance of the Montessori approach in the 21st century.

Montessori today

Montessori's approach has been considered scientific because she used her medical, anthropological and pedagogical knowledge to assess children's development and learning. For her primary research technique she harnessed the power of observation. Whilst her research methods may not have been as rigorous as those of today, we need to acknowledge Montessori's pioneering study of children at the beginning of the 20th century. This was before much of Freud's work was published and certainly before Piaget (1963) or Vygotsky (1978) conducted their research. Some of her statements relating to the nature of children were intuitive, however, their validity has been confirmed subsequently. In his introduction to Lillard's (1980) *Montessori in the Classroom*, Bruner refers to her as both a pragmatist and a mystic. Montessori's commitment to using observation as the key tool for getting to know children cannot be disputed. However, the information she offers about how to document these observations is scant. Equally, she says little about the tools to be used for their analysis. Nonetheless, contemporary observations of children provide us with evidence for the relevance and validity of her approach, particularly if analysed not only in the context of Montessori's own writing but also with reference to theories of developmental psychologists such as Piaget, Vygotsky, Bruner, Bowlby and Erikson.

The continued relevance of Montessori's original findings about children is astounding even though some of her ideas are expressed in rather inaccessible language for today's reader. Perseverance and reflection on her writing, combined with observation and knowledge of children, will lead the reader to a verification of many of the principles underlying

Montessori's approach. In the 1970s Covington Packard explained Montessori's emphasis on learning through practical activities as follows:

> A child gains self-confidence as he feels able to participate usefully in the society around him ... In practical work self-discipline and competence are gradually developed. They come as the child and adult live in mutual respect ... The efforts to attain and successfully accomplish increasingly difficult tasks bring the self-discipline known as self-control. The efforts to respond to one's own needs, to the environmental needs, and to the needs of others, as much as competence allows, bring the kind of self-discipline that is known as responsibility. From this kind of discipline comes a sense of true liberty.
>
> (Covington Packard 1972: 60–61)

Montessori's emphasis on the child's freedom with responsibility remains the key principle of her pedagogy. Without giving children freedom to move and choose, adults would have very little insight into how best to support their learning and development. Opportunities to move freely both inside and outside the classroom guide children towards spontaneous choice, reflecting their interest in the environment and also in social interaction. The selected activities, games and partnerships signal to the adult observer the child's needs as well as interests, and identify support for future learning. This freedom is further supported by extended periods of unstructured time which give the child an opportunity to engage in activities and use their natural pace and rhythm whilst completing them. More will be said about the continuous provision (DfE 2017, BAECE 2012) on offer in Montessori settings in subsequent chapters.

The freedom Montessori speaks about is possible because of the organisation of the learning environment. It needs to be accessible, predictable and consistent as well as interesting to engage the child. Once again, more detail will be given in Chapter 3.

The biggest challenge in ensuring that Montessori's discoveries remain relevant today lies in the attitudes of adults. To give the child the freedom to reveal his/her true potential through self-directed activities requires an adult who is able to not only respect the child, but also trust in the child's innate ability to spontaneously select activities and engage in them, learning through problem solving and discovery. The role of the teacher in Montessori settings, catering for all ages of children, is to guide rather than teach or lead the child in his/her learning. More consideration will be given to this aspect of the Montessori approach when the organisation of Montessori learning is contemplated in Chapter 4.

Key points

1 Montessori was born in Italy in 1870. From her earliest days she was drawn towards sciences at school.
2 She qualified as one of the first women doctors from the University of Rome in 1892.
3 Post qualification she worked with women and children and also in a clinic for children with special needs.
4 Her work in the clinic led her to wanting to know more about how children learned and therefore she enrolled to study educational anthropology. She later lectured in this discipline.
5 She championed the rights of women and children and was asked to set up a nursery for disadvantaged children in the slums of Rome in 1907. She called it Casa dei Bambini – The Children's House.
6 Montessori's experiences and observations of children in this nursery led her to write her first book *The Montessori Method* which was published in 1912.
7 Her approach celebrates the unique potential of each child and advocates a child-centred approach based on the child's freedom to learn within a favourable environment specifically prepared to meet the individual needs of the child.
8 The news of her unique approach spread rapidly and by 1914 she not only established training for teachers interested in her pedagogy but also gained an international reputation.
9 The Montessori approach provides a framework for children's learning and development from birth to eighteen years of age and is international, with at least one Montessori nursery or school in almost every country of the world.
10 Montessori education continues to thrive today because it is based on the innate qualities of children and observation is its main assessment tool.

Reflections

1 Consider the time when Montessori first promoted the rights of women and children:
    ■ how were children perceived at that time?
    ■ what were the rights of women at that time?
    ■ how were young children of the day educated?

2   Research and consider the work of the following prominent early 20th-century pedagogues and see if you can make relevant links with Montessori's principles:
- Rudolf Steiner
- the Macmillan sisters
- Susan Isaacs

3   Consider how Montessori's pedagogical principles reflect or support the work of the following developmental theorists:
- Jean Piaget
- Lev Vygotsky
- Erik Erikson

4   Reflecting on an early years curriculum framework used in your country, such as the EYFS used in England, consider how Montessori principles relate to it in respect of its view of the:
- child
- learning environment
- relationships of children and with adults

5   Considering your own knowledge and understanding of children, which one of the Montessori principles would you:
- like to adopt in your own practice and why?
- find most challenging and why?
- like to share with parents and colleagues and why?

References

BAECE (British Association for Early Childhood Education) (2012) *Development Matters in Early Years Foundation Stage*. London: BAECE.

Covington Packard, R. (1972) *The Hidden Hinge*. Notre Dame: Fides Publishing Inc.

DfE (Department for Education) (2017) *The Early Years Foundation Stage Framework*. London: DfE. Online: www.gov.uk/government/uploads/system/uploads/attachment_data/file/596629/EYFS_STATUTORY_FRAMEWORK_2017.pdf

Edwards, C., Gandini, L. and Forman, G. (1998) *The Hundred Language of Children*, 2nd edn. London: Ablex Publishing Corporation.

Kilpatrick, W. (1914) *The Montessori System Examined*. Boston: Houghton Mifflin.

Kramer, R. (1976) *Maria Montessori*. London: Montessori International Publishing.

Lillard, P.P. (1980) *Montessori in the Classroom*. New York: Schocken Books.

Montessori, M. (1964) [1912] The Montessori Method. New York: Schocken Books.

Montessori, M. (1991) [1918] *The Advanced Montessori Method – Volume 1*. Oxford: ABC – Clio Ltd.

Montessori, M. (1992) [1949] Education and Peace. Oxford: ABC - Clio Ltd, Volume 10.

Montessori, M. (2007a) [1949] *The Absorbent Mind*. Amsterdam: Montessori-Pierson Publishing Company, Volume 1.

Montessori, M. (2007b) [1912] *The Discovery of the Child* (originally published as *The Montessori Method*). Amsterdam: Montessori-Pierson Publishing Company, Volume 2.

Montessori, M. (2007e) [1948] *From Childhood to Adolescence*. Amsterdam: Montessori-Pierson Publishing Company, Volume 12.

Montessori, M. (2007f) [1916] *The Advanced Montessori Method – Volume 2*. Amsterdam: Montessori-Pierson Publishing Company, Volume 13.

MCI (2010) Montessori Philosophy, Module 1. London: MCI.

Montessori, M. (2012) *The 1946 London Lectures*. Amsterdam: Montessori-Pierson Publishing Company, Volume 17.

Piaget, J. (1963) *The Psychology of Intelligence*. Totowa, NJ: Littlefield Adams.

Standing, E.M. (1984) *Maria Montessori, Her Life and Work*. New York: Plume.

Vygotsky, L. (1978) *Mind in Society*. Cambridge, MA: Harvard University Press.

2 Montessori's view of child development

This chapter explains Montessori's view of children's development. Knowledge and understanding of her approach are essential for all those who work with children in Montessori settings. Practitioners use her developmental perspective to interpret observations of children and apply this knowledge to the planning of activities, changes of the learning environment and teaching strategies used when working in Montessori classrooms.

According to Montessori the development of the child during the first three years after birth is unequalled in intensity and importance:

> If we consider the transformations, adaptations, achievements and conquests of the environment during the first period of life from zero to three years, it is functionally a longer period that all the following periods put together from three years until death. For this reason, these three years may be considered to be as long as a whole life.
>
> (Montessori 1989a: 19)

'If education is to be based on what we know of little children, we must first understand their development,' wrote Montessori (2012: 23), and following the biological development of human beings, Montessori (2007a) organised children's development in three six-year periods: birth to six, six to twelve and twelve to eighteen, and further determined these by the loss of, first, the milk teeth around the age of six, and of molars around the age of twelve (Montessori 2007e). Each of these periods is further subdivided into three-year spans. Before we discuss spans in more detail, it is important to point out that Montessori was one of the first pedagogues to advocate the importance of the first six years of life. From her perspective, they were far more important than the university years. They lay a firm foundation for the whole future of the child, both in attitudes to social aspects of life and to learning. During these formative years the child also establishes conceptual frameworks based on sensory experiences, which, according to Montessori (2007a, 2007b) are essential precursors of all academic learning at school and university.

The Absorbent Mind (birth to six years of age)

Impressions pour into us and we store them in our minds ... the child undergoes a transformation. Impressions do not merely enter the mind; they form it. They incarnate themselves in him ... We have a name for this type of mentality – the Absorbent Mind.

(Montessori 2007a: 24)

The Absorbent Mind begins to function in the womb, when new experiences are stored in a special kind of unconscious memory which Montessori (2007a, 2007b) named the *Mneme.* The Mneme is closely linked with *human tendencies* – genetic predispositions that determine our unique human characteristics such as the ability to orientate ourselves and explore our environment, the ability to communicate, the capacity for exactitude, gregariousness, creativity and imagination. These human tendencies unfold as the child matures; they are manifested in the child's sensitive periods. Montessori (2007a) called the first stage of the child's development the *Absorbent Mind* because it is at this stage that children absorb information from their environment effortlessly and with ease. This ease of learning is not matched in subsequent developmental stages. She believed that this absorption was possible because of the child's inner drive, which she called the *Horme* (2007a). The Horme drives the child's special sensitivity to his/her environment which she termed *sensitive periods*. This latter term she borrowed from the Dutch scientist Hugo de Vries (Montessori 1966), whom she met during her time in Amsterdam between the two world wars. Montessori explained that:

A child's different inner sensibilities enable him to choose from his complex environment what is suitable and necessary for his growth. They make the child sensitive to some things, but leave him indifferent to others. When a particular sensitiveness is aroused in a child, it is like a light that shines on some objects but not on others, making of them his whole world.

(Montessori 1966: 42)

The key sensitive periods during the Absorbent Mind stage are: *sensitivity to order, movement, small detail and language, refinement of the senses* and *sensitivity to social aspects.* They are not sequential; instead they overlap and grow in prominence as the child matures. If nurtured, the child blossoms in specific areas of development, such a movement or language. When the sensitive period is satisfied, it subsides. According to Montessori (2007a, 2007b), if the opportunities to support these special times in the child's first six years of life are not met, the child will not be able to acquire these skills with the same ease in the future, and chances for optimum development will be missed.

Spiritual embryonic stage (also referred to as the Unconscious Absorbent Mind)

> The child ... is a spiritual embryo which needs its own special environment. Just as a physical embryo needs its mother's womb in which to grow, so the spiritual embryo needs to be protected by an external environment that is warm with love and rich in nourishments, where everything is disposed to welcome, and nothing to harm it.
>
> (Montessori 1966: 34)

The spiritual embryonic stage is in evidence during the first three years of the child's life. Experiences during the first year of the child's life are most powerful and affect the child's whole being. Montessori also referred to this stage as the *Unconscious Absorbent Mind.* During this period the child's experiences continue to be stored in the *Mneme,* a special 'kind of memory, which does not consciously remember, but absorbs images into the individual's very life' (Montessori 2007a: 57). The key feature of this stage of development is the need for independence. Montessori (2007a: 96–97) states, 'The child's first characteristic is to carry out his actions by himself, without anyone helping him.'

This stage is characterised by the child's unfolding personality and emergence of the human potential. The child's sensitive periods for order, movement, language and small objects are prominent. These sensitive periods manifest themselves in a pattern of behaviour. For example, a characteristic of such a period is the repeated performance of some actions for no apparent reason. Following such activity a new function emerges, often with extraordinary force. During these periods the child shows vitality and pleasure in performing these actions. A child in a deprived environment which lacks stimulation, or a child who is obstructed at this time of his learning, may display negative behaviours, and according to Montessori his/her natural development may be thwarted.

Montessori (1966) believed that the sensitive periods were not only an aid to the child's inner development or *psychic life*, but also an important aspect of his learning process. Therefore, in formulating her approach to education, Montessori acknowledged the importance of these periods of time when the child learned certain things more easily than at any other time. Montessori teachers use their observations and understanding of the sensitive periods as tools in organising and preparing the favourable environment and in planning children's learning. Standing writes in *Maria Montessori: Her Life and Work*: 'When the education of children is organised in relation to their sensitive periods, they work with a sustained enthusiasm which has to be seen in order to be believed' (Standing 1984: 133).

A period for sensitivity to *order*

This is one of the first sensitive periods to appear. It shows itself in the first month of life. The whole development of the child is directly related to his/her need for, and love of, order. Order in the child's external environment helps him/her to categorise perceptions and to make sense of the world. It also makes children feel secure and supports their exploration and orientation. Montessori quotes many instances of very young children being disturbed and upset by the lack of order in their environment. For example, exposure to unfamiliar places and people can be disturbing to them. This need for *inner orientation* (Montessori 1966) in the first year of life is supported by predictable routines as well as an orderly external environment. For example, a young child will recognise the signs of food preparation – and will often respond to them with great excitement. However, this need, or striving, for order in the child's environment must not be confused with the adults' need for tidy surroundings. It is more that the child needs a consistent, stable and predictable environment for normal development: 'It is necessary for the child to have this order and stability in his environment because he is constructing himself out of the elements of the environment ... it is his foundation' (Standing 1984: 125–126).

The need for order is particularly evident in the child from about one and a half years. This coincides with the stage in her/his development when she or he is first able to manipulate the environment and move objects from one place to another. She expects to find objects where she first saw them and will go to great lengths to put them back if they are 'out of place'. This striving for order is a characteristic of the child in the first stage of development, the Absorbent Mind. Order in a Montessori school is a very important aspect of the environment and supports children's learning and development.

A sensitivity for *movement*

This sensitive period begins in the womb when the embryo begins to stretch and move. It continues from the moment of birth, with the baby turning his/her head, grasping objects with the hands and feet, putting them into the mouth, rolling over, crawling, sitting, standing and finally walking. This is the height of this sensitive period, and the ability to walk facilitates exploration of a wider environment.

From approximately one year, when most children learn to walk, they have a need to practise and perfect the skill. Adults walk to get from one place to another, i.e. they have a goal, but the child at this stage walks for the sake of it. Once mobile she/he is constantly on the move. Mothers and carers often comment on their toddlers spending an hour going up and down stairs. We tend to underestimate the child's stamina to walk. Children of two and three are capable of walking long distances provided they can do it at their own pace.

The need for movement and physical activity must be considered when providing an environment for young children. Toddlers must be given opportunities to move freely and safely. They also need to carry, transport, pull and push objects, so strengthening the upper part of their bodies, as well as developing a sense of balance and spatial awareness. The refinement of movement, particularly of hand movements, is an important element in the child's progression towards growing independence as the child approaches the second sub-stage of the Absorbent Mind. To develop all aspects of their mobility, young children need time, space and opportunities to practise their newly emerging skills.

Movement is not to be regarded as 'letting off steam' but as a key component of learning. A young child will not develop fully if she/he is immobilised by sedentary activities.

A sensitivity for *small objects*

At around six months, when the child becomes more mobile and therefore has a larger environment to explore, she/he becomes drawn to small objects, e.g., small insects, pebbles, stones, blades of grass. Montessori (1966) gives examples of her observations of children of this age having an urge to pay attention to detail. When out walking, a child will stop many times to examine some tiny detail in his/her path. This is part of the child's effort to build up an understanding of the world. The fascination with detail is not surprising when you consider the young child's size in relation to the environment inhabited by adults. Montessori likens the child's experiences to those of Gulliver reaching the land of the Lilliputs. From the examples Montessori gives, we can see how the child's focus on objects, particularly tiny detail, at this stage of his/her development supports emerging cognitive skills linking to his/her actions and speech.

A period of sensitivity to *language*

The child's ability to use language is of major importance. Language and activity play a vital role in subsequent intellectual or cognitive growth. The sensitive period for language also begins in the womb. We now have research evidence that babies in the womb are sensitive to their mother's voice and recognise familiar sounds. This sensitivity to language, particularly the language of the prime carer, is present from the moment of birth and continues until about the age of five years. By this age, most children, with virtually no direct teaching, learn basic sentence patterns and achieve considerable mastery in the use of at least one language.

This does not mean that a child of five years has full language competence. She/he continues to acquire more complex sentence structures during the primary school years provided the basic language has been achieved during the sensitive period. The development of language is the most striking example of a sensitive period. Although she/he cannot speak at birth, the baby is 'tuned in' to language above all other sounds. When she/he begins to make babbling noises she/he does not imitate the washing machine or the telephone but makes the sounds of human speech:

> so it may be that this powerful hearing mechanism only responds and acts in relation to sounds of a particular kind – those of speech. The result is that words heard by the child set in motion the complicated mechanisms by which he makes the movements needed to reproduce them.
>
> (Montessori 2007a: 107)

Because of his/her special sensitivity to speech, the baby unconsciously concentrates his/her attention on the structure of language and absorbs it without difficulty, no matter how complex it is. In a multilingual household the child can assimilate two languages simultaneously, provided they are clearly differentiated by the people speaking them.

If, for any reason, a child is not exposed to language during the sensitive period, she/he will be irrevocably damaged. Depending upon the degree of deprivation, she/he will suffer limitations in her/his intellectual growth that can never be totally compensated for. There are many tragic examples of children who, during the sensitive period, have been isolated from society. One example, documented in *The Wild Boy of Aveyron* (Itard 1801), deals with a boy who was found at the age of approximately eleven years living in a forest in France. Although he became relatively socialised and humanised, he never acquired full language competence. The role of adults and peers in children's growing language skills cannot be underestimated. The need to hear and absorb rich language in an everyday context is of paramount importance if we want to foster the child's capacity for effective communication.

As with other sensitive periods, Montessori education takes advantage of the child's interest in language to provide materials and activities to develop vocabulary, to introduce grammar and reading as well as to give opportunities for the expression and sharing of ideas and feelings. The child at the stage of the Unconscious Absorbent Mind is entirely egocentric – driven by the *Horme* to see the world from his/her own perspective, unable to consider or understand the needs of others.

Social embryonic stage (also referred to as the Conscious Absorbent Mind)

Gradually, around the age of three, the *social embryonic stage* emerges – the child begins to demonstrate the ability to control his/her volition and becomes interested in social conventions and aspects of his/her culture. Montessori (2007a: 222) describes it as 'the embryonic period for the formation of character and society'. The social child emerges at the end of this stage – a child capable of empathy, socially adept and independent, ready for formal education. The two key sensitive periods are refinement of the senses and social aspects of life.

A period of sensitivity for the *refinement of the senses*

The young child has a natural curiosity to explore the environment. At about the age when she or he begins to crawl, the exploration often takes the form of picking up objects and putting them in the mouth. The child is not only tasting – she/he is beginning to coordinate interaction between all his separate senses. There is strong evidence that the effects produced by the stimulation of a given sense organ are continuously modified by ongoing activities using other senses. The development of this inter-sensory judgement goes on up to the age of eight years and can be improved or refined by guided experience and teaching. The quality of stimulation and activities in the environment have a direct bearing on the degree of sense discrimination that the child attains; for example, Montessori teachers have shown that children who work with colour tablets (Chapter 5) can achieve a degree of discrimination in distinguishing subtle colour variation that many adults never attain.

From a very early age a child begins to make selected responses to sense stimuli, i.e. she/he only hears, sees, touches, tastes and smells that which she/he wants to. This selectivity of response is necessary to prevent the human nervous system from being overwhelmed by stimuli. It also has the effect of making previous experience the key to what a human selects in his/her response.

Whilst Montessori (1966) recognised the importance of sensory experiences from the moment of birth, she placed particular emphasis upon the importance of helping the child to make *sensory discrimination* and the *refinement of the senses*. Much of her well-known teaching apparatus (Chapter 5) is concerned with ways of improving the refinement of the child's senses. With most children this experience of sensory discrimination is given during the pre-school period from about two to five years of age and forms the foundation for much of later learning in Montessori classrooms.

The sensitive period for refinement of the senses is most prominent around the age of three, when the child has the mental capacity to begin to build upon the myriad of sensory experiences gained during the stage of the *Unconscious Absorbent Mind* (spiritual embryonic stage) which are logged in his/her *Mneme*. At this stage she/he begins to organise the sensory impressions with the help of activities which categorise these impressions, such as sorting, matching and pairing, making patterns and classifying. Montessori developed materials which aid this process and are presented to the child in the sensorial area of the classroom and in the cultural area (knowledge of world; see Chapter 5). These activities, alongside the practical life activities, provide the foundation of all future learning in Montessori classrooms.

A sensitivity to the *social aspects* of life

At about three years of age, children become more aware and ready to be part of a group. This is why, traditionally, most nursery education starts at around this age. If given the opportunity, children begin to cooperate with other children, form early friendships and grow in awareness of the needs of others. With the help of growing language skills they begin to imitate and use social mores and culturally appropriate behaviours.

In Montessori nurseries there is a growing sense of cohesion which Montessori (2007a) maintains is not instilled by instruction but comes about spontaneously and is directed by an unconscious power – the human tendency for gregariousness and communication. The process of cooperation between children does not suddenly come about, this is a gradual process of maturation.

The development of manners and social skills is promoted by Montessori teachers at this time to enhance the child's interest in being part of his/her society. The customs of his/her culture bond her/him to the community. His/her sensitivity to 'appropriate' modes of behaviour allows the child to fit into the group to which she/he belongs. The child's sensitivity to social aspects and growing maturity are supported by the vertical grouping (Montessori 2007a) of the classroom. In an ideal environment children between the ages of three and six are grouped together; the classroom represents a family situation where children support each other in learning and in creating a cohesive social unit (Montessori 2007a).

The child who has experienced social cohesion, where each child is seen as a unique individual, and who is able to consider the needs of others, is a child on the cusp of childhood – a child entering a new stage of development.

Childhood (six to twelve years of age)

Montessori (2007e) considered this stage of the child's development to be the most productive and calm, during which the child embraces social life with enthusiasm and new energy. At this stage, the child is ready for wider experiences and education needs to satisfy not only his/her curiosity and keenness to acquire knowledge, but also the need to belong to a group and exercise his/her growing moral awareness. The key sensitive periods are those for acquisition of culture and morality. This stage is, once again, subdivided: ages six to nine and nine to twelve. Montessori did not describe specific characteristics of these sub-stages. However, in well-established Montessori primary schools, children are divided into classes according to these two stages in order to reflect their growing academic and intellectual ability.

Adolescence (twelve to eighteen years of age)

For Montessori (2007e), this stage is characterised by its volatile nature which requires, as in the case of the first stage of the child's life, a very understanding adult to support the young person. This is particularly so during the first sub-stage, which Montessori termed puberty, when the child's body undergoes tremendous physical changes. During the second sub-phase, the young adult has a need to identify with his/her social group. Montessori advocated a revolutionary approach to the education of teenagers which is described in Appendix 1.

Key points

1 The Montessori approach is based on a recognition of the unique nature of each individual.
2 Montessori's medical background led her to establishing a universal pedagogy which is designed to support the needs of each individual, whilst facilitating a social transformation.
3 Children develop in stages (divided into three six-year spans), each with its unique characteristics and needs.
4 Children's sensitive periods are key tools which guide teachers and parents in organising appropriate activities to support learning and development.
5 Montessori's approach is based on children's active learning; movement is seen as the key to cognitive development.
6 Children develop competence and independence and refine their senses by using specifically developed activities and materials.
7 Social relationships unfold as children mature and grow in their knowledge of social conventions and embrace the positive examples set by adults and older peers.

8 Freedom to learn combined with responsibility for one's actions lead the child towards self-discipline, social awareness and pro-social behaviour. For Montessori, these are the foundations of the individual's true liberty.

9 Observation is the key tool for the evaluation of children's learning and development and guides the teacher in planning appropriate activities.

10 Appropriately trained and educated adults must trust and respect the uniqueness of each individual child.

Reflections

1 Consider the unique characteristics of one of your key children with respect to:
- his/her physical skills
- language ability and cognitive understanding
- social ability and emotional well-being

2 Having made these considerations, what could you do to:
- enhance the learning environment?
- facilitate new learning?
- promote social interactions for the child?

3 Reread the aims and objectives of your setting and consider:
- how these relate to the aims of the Montessori approach
- in view of these aims, would you like to make changes and why?
- how would you go about discussing these proposed changes with your colleagues?

4 Reflect on the observations you make in your setting and consider how they affect your practice. How do they contribute to your knowledge and understanding of:
- the children?
- the learning environment?
- yourself and your colleagues?

5 Reflect on your understanding of the child's 'work' and 'play':
- consider the value you place on each
- consider your role in facilitating work and play
- do you trust and respect the child's choices of activity and why?

References

Itard, J.M. Gaspard (1801) *The Wild Boy of Aveyron*. Online: https://owlcation.com/social-sciences/The-Wild-Boy-of-Aveyron

Montessori, M. (1966) [1936] *The Secret of Childhood*. Notre Dame, IN: Fides Publishers Ltd.

Montessori, M. (1989a) [1961] *What You Should Know About Your Child*. Oxford: ABC – Clio Ltd, Volume 4.

Montessori, M. (2007a) *The Absorbent Mind*. Amsterdam: Montessori-Pierson Publishing Company, Volume 1.

Montessori, M. (2007b) *The Discovery of the Child* (originally published as *The Montessori Method*). Amsterdam: Montessori-Pierson Publishing Company, Volume 2.

Montessori, M. (2007e) *From Childhood to Adolescence*. Amsterdam: Montessori-Pierson Publishing Company, Volume 12.

Montessori, M. (2012) *The 1946 London Lectures*. Amsterdam: Montessori-Pierson Publishing Company.

Standing E.M. (1984) *Maria Montessori, Her Life and Work*. New York: Plume.

3 Organisation of Montessori schools

This chapter elaborates on the principles which underpin Montessori education across the age groups. It gives examples of the organisation of Montessori schools around the world. It explores the structure of a typical day in a Montessori setting and the differences between a day in a setting for babies and toddlers, nursery and primary-school-age children. Lastly, it explains how areas of learning are organised in the classroom and how this organisation impacts the role of the teacher as the child grows older.

> This is education, understood as a help to life; an education from birth, which feeds a peaceful revolution and unites all in a common aim ... Mothers, fathers, politicians: all must combine in their respect and help this delicate work of formation, which the little child carriers on ... under the tutelage of the inner guide.
>
> (Montessori 2007a: 15–16)

Montessori context

As mentioned in the previous chapter, Montessori believed that children develop in unique stages and these are reflected in the organisation of the Montessori provision for children. The underlining principles, based on Montessori's early discoveries, of nurturing the child's individual potential, supporting independence and offering freedom within limits in order to foster responsibility should apply to all Montessori settings irrespective of whether they cater to babies, toddlers, pre-schoolers, primary or secondary-school-age children. However, how these principles are interpreted depends upon the children's developmental needs and levels of maturity. The culture and regulatory requirements of the country in which the Montessori nurseries and schools operate also determine their organisational structure. This chapter aims to explain how Montessori provision is organised in practice.

The majority of the 22,000 Montessori schools around the world provide education for children between the ages of two/three and six. Most of them are private businesses or charitable trusts established for the purpose of delivering Montessori education to children. Montessori herself did not patent or protect the name as a trademark and therefore the movement is unregulated; as a result, a wide range of Montessori practice can be observed around the world. However, there are common features which should be maintained in the majority of Montessori schools. These include the use of Montessori learning materials and the organisation of the learning environment. The principles, discussed above, should underpin the schools' practice. Unfortunately, there are also settings which still adopt the Montessori name to attract parents and use it as a marketing tool without actually employing any trained teachers or using Montessori equipment.

Montessori training and practice

The code of practice used in Montessori nurseries and schools around the world is linked with the training organisation where the current owners and managers studied. There are several international Montessori awarding bodies which set their own training curricula and assessment procedures based on Montessori's legacy and original writing. However, the interpretation of her text is unique to each organisation, despite many similarities. These organisations have also developed quality assurance procedures for the schools associated with them and operate a range of accreditation schemes. Among the key international players in Montessori teacher training are the:

- American Montessori Society (AMS), the key organisation influencing and directing training in the United States. The courses delivered under its auspices comply with the regulatory standards set by the Montessori Accreditation Council for Teacher Education (MACTE) and meet the federal requirements for teacher education. In recent years AMS-validated courses have been delivered outside the US, primarily in China and some countries in Eastern Europe.
- Association Montessori Internationale (AMI), with its headquarters in Amsterdam, which sees itself as the protector of the Montessori legacy

and offers courses internationally. It holds an archive of Montessori's writing and the original designs for Montessori equipment. In recent years it has also established a serious of outreach projects, such as Educateurs Sans Frontieres.

■ Montessori St. Nicholas, established in London in 1946, was the first organisation to promote Montessori training by correspondence and so disseminate knowledge and awareness of the Montessori approach to parts of the world where it would not have been accessible in any other way. Since 1998 the charity's training has been delivered by Montessori Centre International (MCI). In September 2014 MCI launched the first Montessori qualification which is fully integrated with the English national standards for early years educators. This qualification is externally validated and included on Ofqual's list. MCI also offers a foundation degree with progression route to bachelors and masters programmes. The MCI courses are delivered via a virtual learning environment which facilitates an international learning community across all modes of study and promotes partnership and cooperation amongst MCI students and graduates.

Much effort has been made by all these organisations to ensure that the training and qualifications are accepted nationally and internationally, but the fact that there is not one body to represent Montessori pedagogy and practice has continued to complicate their efforts.

The interpretation of the principles which inform Montessori practice is debated within the Montessori community and is deeply influenced by the approach adopted by the various training organisations educating Montessori teachers around the world. As a result, graduates from Montessori Centre International, American Montessori Society or the Association Montessori Internationale will interpret children's behaviours, use of materials and sense of liberty from slightly different perspectives. This can either lead to rich debate and meaningful application of the approach to children's learning or to isolation. For the Montessori approach to remain relevant and available to children, dialogue within the Montessori community and with national and international colleagues in the field of pedagogy is essential. It is the author's belief that opening up of the Montessori approach to current research in all aspects of developmental psychology and current trends in pedagogy would be beneficial to all who engage in such discourse.

International Montessori education

The reason for private ownership of many Montessori nurseries and schools is linked with the fact that they offer provision for children of a pre-school age, prior to the compulsory education funded by many countries. The Netherlands funds Montessori primary education and there are Montessori public schools in the US which are financed by the individual states. European countries such as Sweden, Germany and Austria also part fund schools that wish to follow the Montessori curriculum. In recent years several countries have provided opportunities for Montessori education to be introduced. For example the Czech government has funded several nurseries and primary schools, whilst the Bulgarian government provided for introduction of the Montessori approach in some of its primary schools and the Saudi government has piloted and funded a large number of Montessori nurseries in Jeddah. The Tibetan government's schools operating in north India all use Montessori materials, particularly the literacy and numeracy materials, to support young children's learning in these areas. In all these countries the Montessori schools must satisfy the requirements of local education boards. The schools must ensure that their Montessori curricula meet the local regulatory and educational requirements, particularly at the primary and secondary levels of education. This should also lead to children from Montessori settings becoming prepared for national tests and examinations. Generally, children attending Montessori schools fare well in these tests and demonstrate that, apart from being academically able, they also display positive attitudes to learning, initiative and respect for themselves, others and the environment. There are many Montessori school owners and teachers who feel the less structured and more open approach to learning, not dominated by preparations for examinations, is of benefit to children and their attitude to learning.

Montessori schools in the UK

In the past ten years there have been several opportunities for Montessori education to be delivered in mainstream schools in England, with the Gorton Mount Primary School, now in new premises and called Rushbrook Primary School, in Manchester and the Stebbing Primary School in Essex pioneering the way with strong leadership and financial and academic support from the Montessori St. Nicholas charity. More recently the Aldersbrook Primary School in Wanstead has demonstrated the benefits of the Montessori approach introduced in its nursery and reception classes and this has prompted further interest in several local schools and provided a model for other schools interested in this approach. The recent initiatives continue to be supported by Montessori St. Nicholas charity by offering suitable training and guidance on preparation of the learning environment.

Nursery/school organisation

To get a firmer grasp of the organisation of Montessori settings it is important to link the learning environment with the developmental needs of children and acknowledge Montessori's commitment to establishing learning communities where children of several ages are grouped together in an effort to reflect a family. The key advantages of this approach lie in the fact that children can learn from one another. The younger children find the older children a great inspiration, while the older children benefit by using their knowledge to demonstrate, explain or problem solve with the younger children. This benefits both the consolidation of their knowledge as well as the growth of self-esteem; they enjoy being the 'teachers'. Montessori explained that:

> Our schools are live. To understand what the older ones are doing fills the little ones with enthusiasm. The older ones are happy to be able to teach what they know. There are no inferiority complexes, but everyone achieves a healthy normality through the mutual exchange of spiritual energy.
>
> (Montessori 2007a: 207)

For the pre-school age child, the ideal Montessori setting is organised as follows: birth to three – babies and toddlers, often referred to as an 'infant community', and three to six – nursery school/kindergarten, sometimes called 'casa' with reference to Montessori's original name for the schools catering for this age group. As children get older, primary or elementary schools usually have two classrooms: for six to nine and nine to twelve year olds, reflecting the children's growing academic ability. Meanwhile, the teenagers attending Montessori school usually share their learning but follow individual paths of study; academic as well as practical work is promoted in the learning of these young people. Secondary-school-age children are referred to by Montessori (2007e) as Erdkinder children (or 'Earth children').

Infant community – environment and organisation

These environments are usually on offer in settings providing full daycare for working parents, meaning that the children will stay at nursery the whole day, often from 8 am until 6 pm. Some settings also offer mother/carer and toddler groups which give 18–30-month-old children the opportunity to become familiar with a Montessori setting whilst accompanied by their prime or secondary carers. These groups often offer one or two sessions each week not lasting longer than two hours.

Babies

The children's developmental needs are the main focus of this provision. Appropriate care, both physical and emotional, is at the forefront of the carer's/practitioner's daily concerns. The children's sensitive periods for order, movement, language and small details are observed by practitioners as they prepare an appropriate environment. In most infant communities the babies and toddlers will be together in a spacious room with access to the outdoors. Provision is made for changing and sleeping as well as food preparation. The practitioners focus on children's individual daily routines and, where possible, these routines mirror the child's home experiences to maintain consistency. These routines are communicated daily to parents, either verbally or with the help of a day book, in which sleeping patterns, food intake, bowel motions and the activities enjoyed by the child are recorded. The book is also used by parents to share information and concerns about their children with the nursery. Dedicated adults who know each child individually will ensure continuity of routines and also satisfy the children's sensitivity to order in their sleeping, eating and changing arrangements. Where possible, the children take a nap and eat according to their individual body clock rather than in an organised routine set by the nursery. In discussion with parents, the children will be introduced to solid food and given opportunities to feed themselves. Practitioners are aware of children's sensitive period for language and therefore babies experience the natural rhythm of communication, books, songs and rhymes as part of the essential foundation for their language development. Daily outdoor experiences are also a part of the nursery provision for all babies. Many nurseries in England also include treasure baskets into their range of resources for sensory exploration.

Toddlers

All toddlers need considerable floor space to practise their standing and walking. For this reason the room will be uncluttered and the floor carpeted. They are encouraged to feed themselves and, when ready, the setting will instigate potty training in partnership with parents. The children will be given opportunities to help with snack preparation, develop good habits of washing hands and put on their shoes and coats for outdoor play.

Singing and books are a part of the daily routine, as are opportunities to engage with posting, pushing and pulling activities and puzzles. The older toddlers will be introduced to pouring their own drink and will be expected to feed themselves. They are encouraged to walk and climb. This is in support of their sensitive period for movement, which requires the development of the whole body. Gross and fine body movements are involved, as well as opportunities to develop balance and spatial aware-ness through activities such as riding bikes, negotiating stairs and using ramps and slides. Toddlers also engage their arms and hands when mani-pulating puzzles, blocks and books. They also have access to heuristic play involving bags of objects which can be carried and provide for sorting of everyday objects. Lastly, they help with domestic tasks such as clearing their plates after a snack or lunch and helping to wash up and clean up.

Toddler's learning activities are organised on open shelves and they are free to choose what they wish to do. This is a fundamental feature of all Montessori learning environments which enables children to make choices, and they are encouraged to put the activities back on the shelf after use. Well-spoken language is essential in promoting children's sensitive period for language, which is at its height during the second and third year of life.

Organisation of the day

The toddlers' day usually starts with breakfast, followed by indoor and outdoor activities, lunch and sleep in the afternoon before more activities are available. In many daycare settings the children are also offered an evening meal before they go home. It often seems that the daily routine of the very young children is dominated by their meal times. This can be minimised with the morning and/or afternoon snack being available when the child is ready. This encourages another level of independence and decision making and follows the natural rhythms of the child.

The curriculum for this age group is guided by the need to move, explore through the senses and engage in communication. Some early

Montessori activities such as those developed by the Montessori manufacturer Nienhuis and recommended by Montanaro (1991) and Lillard and Lillard Jensen (2003) may be on offer in addition to opportunities to look after the nursery garden, play in the sandpit and with water and experiment with an easel and mark-making tools.

Nursery environments and organisation

Ideally, when entering nursery young children are around three years old and able to be independent of adult help in their toileting, eating and dressing needs. They should also be capable of expressing their basic needs verbally and asking for what they need. If they have progressed from the infant community, they will already be able to choose activities from the open shelves and return them. If they are newcomers to the setting, they will first learn the new routines which are part of the classroom etiquette – where to put their coats and shoes, how to greet their teachers and friends, where to wash their hands, how to roll and unroll a work mat and how to choose an activity and return it to the shelf.

Nursery-age children should be able to demonstrate some emotional autonomy and be able to spend some time without their prime carer and relate to all the adults in the nursery. The classroom will be organised according to areas of learning or, depending on the children attending and the space available, the areas of learning may be organised in different rooms for the children to move freely from one room to another. Freedom to move, choose and express one's ideas are at the heart of the organisation of the nursery learning environment. The focus remains on the sensitive periods so evident in the toddler age: order, movement, small detail and language, with special attention paid to the refinement of the senses and social aspects of life. In fact, in all aspects of the child's development Montessori practitioners now look for refinement and fine tuning of skills and greater knowledge and understanding of their environment.

The children of this age group thrive in an orderly classroom because order promotes freedom of choice; they refine their gross and fine motor skills as they learn to hop and skip, use the outdoor equipment with confidence and commence riding a bike unaided by adults or stabilisers. Their balance and spatial awareness also increase as they become better coordinated. Their fine motor skills improve and they begin to be capable of cutting, holding a pencil and enjoying all kinds of craft activities including sewing. They also begin to experiment with language by making rhymes and using unusual words. Their interest in books and understanding of how books work increases and they begin to narrate the stories from their favourite books and to write their name. During all these activities they notice small changes in the organisation of the environment and rejoice in sharing these changes with their friends and adults.

The Montessori environment provides children with opportunities to refine their senses by using the specifically designed Montessori materials and games. These activities help to establish the foundations of conceptual understanding by organising and classifying experiences and exploration of the materials. As children grow in social awareness they establish their first friendships and learn the social conventions of their culture with the help of their peers and adults, who serve as positive role models.

Organisation of the nursery day

To satisfy sensitive periods for order, movement, language, small detail, refinement of the senses and social aspects of life as well as the child's growing ability to concentrate, the day is usually organised into three-hour blocks of activity which Montessori (1991) termed *work-cycles*. In practice, this means that from the beginning of the nursery day children should be free to select activities of interest. They are also expected to return them to the right place. Montessorians refer to this as the *cycle of activity* (Montessori 1991, MCI 2010). The cycle of activity begins and finishes at the shelf where the material is stored. This applies to both the indoor and outdoor environment.

During the work-cycle there may be times when the child is engaged inside and outside the classroom and when they participate in a small group lesson such as story time, music or yoga. These are sometimes delivered by peripatetic teachers. Children might also engage in a one-to-one lesson given by the teacher. All activities which are spontaneously chosen by the child, including the snack and outdoor play, are valued as part of his/her learning. For the younger child (three to four years old), the work-cycle consists of many cycles of activity, whilst the older children (five to six years old) may engage in one or two prolonged activities or games. There are also some children who learn better by observing others engaged in activities. They only touch the learning materials when they have observed and absorbed all the processes or steps essential for success-ful completion of the given activity. The Montessori teacher will observe this child carefully; his/her body language will indicate engagement or 'just passing of time'. Thus the teacher will either leave the child alone or try to engage him/her in some activity which may be deemed appropriate, based on previous observation which identifies the child's interest or an area for development.

Children who attend nursery for the morning or afternoon sessions only may stay for lunch, which they share with their friends and teachers, either prepared by the setting or by their parents and carers. Children who stay for the day may spend the afternoon work-cycle engaged in more spontaneous activities selected from the activities offered in the favourable environment, or may participate in more organised activities such as dance lessons or second language lessons. The younger children may also rest after lunch, depending on the culture of the setting. Some settings offer a choice of morning or afternoon sessions, in which case the afternoon programme mirrors the morning activities.

Ideally, there will be free access to the outdoor and indoor learning environments; both areas having activities beneficial to the child, planned and appropriately supported by the adults. Montessori practitioners believe it is important that at nursery children refine their senses, are introduced to literacy and numeracy, extend their knowledge of the world and have access to a wide range of creative activities. The freedom within the favourable environment supports their autonomy and emerging initiative (Erikson 1940).

Primary environments and organisation of the day

Children who progress from Montessori nurseries onto primary education, around the age of six, are used to making choices and taking responsibility for their actions. They find the transition easy because, once again, activities are accessible and available, reflecting the children's interests and sensitive periods. The freedom of choice remains, but the expectations are that the child engages in some literacy task and mathematical activity every day. These activities are usually discussed with the teacher either on a weekly or daily basis and a plan is prepared. This plan is available to the child, who is able to check it and decide how to progress with the planned task.

In addition to literacy and numeracy, the child also follows a project topic which relates to biology, geography or history. These project topics are organised in what Montessori termed the Five Great Lessons (more information is given in the following chapters) and they give children the opportunity to research and learn about topics of interest and reinforce their literacy, numeracy and problem-solving skills. It is up to the child when he/she completes the tasks on the list, provided it is within the set timeframe. This means that some children will complete the literacy and numeracy tasks as quickly as possible in order to be free to continue in their project research, whilst others will procrastinate or start the day with the project topic. Whilst they are establishing this new routine, the teacher reminds and guides the children in completing their plan of action. The work-cycle of three to four hours continues, but as the activities now take longer, it is possible that a child engaged in extended literacy tasks may leave his/her work by labelling it with their name whilst they go to take a snack or have a run outside if there is free access to the outdoor classroom.

Primary-school-age children actively participate in the daily upkeep of the classroom and are either able to select or are allotted a specific domestic task for a day or the week, such as emptying the rubbish bins at the end of the day, helping with preparation of snacks or lunch, sweeping and dusting, watering classroom plants or the vegetable patch and feeding any animals the school may keep and look after. Unlike the nursery-age children, who would have done many of these tasks under the supervision of an adult, the primary-school-age children do them as part of their daily routine. The tasks are part of the social aspect of the learning community, to which children are expected to contribute, and reflect their sensitive period for moral and social aspects of life.

The role of the Montessori teacher

She is the main connecting link between the material ... and the child.
(Montessori 2007b: 151)

the teacher teaches little and observes much, and above all, it is her function to direct the psychic activity of the children and their physiological development. For this reason I have changed the name of the teacher into that of directress.
(Montessori 1965: 174)

In her writing, Montessori (2007a, 2007b) describes the teacher as the *directress/director*. She refers to them more as a film director than a teacher. However, in recent years, the use of this word has been challenged by many in the Montessori community (Loeffler 1992). To 'direct' still implies to be in control of the child's learning, whereas in the contemporary context her/his role has been interpreted to mean more of a guide or facilitator.

For the child to be able to access spontaneous learning, she/he requires an environment favourably prepared to meet individual needs and interests. It is the role of the Montessori teacher to prepare a learning environment which corresponds to the developmental needs of the age group and reflects the interests of the children attending the class. Observation is the key tool for identification of necessary changes in the environment as well as potential modification of the layout or content of the classroom.

To meet this challenge, teachers first need to know:

- about children's development, both from the Montessori point of view as well as from the perspective of developmental research. They also need to ensure that their knowledge in this area is current and relevant to their practice;
- about the Montessori learning materials, their use and benefits and the principles which underpin them. This knowledge and understanding will enable them to develop or purchase materials and activities designed by Montessori herself as well as those which complement, enhance or further develop the children's knowledge, understanding and skill set;
- how to observe and document children's learning. Progress within the Montessori pedagogical approach is based on individual knowledge of children and planning for their specific needs and interests in support of their development;
- how to place the needs of the child above their own needs as a teacher, in the sense that it must be the child who leads the learning and the adult who supports it, not the other way around;
- how to organise and maintain the classroom according to children's abilities;
- how to relate to colleagues and parents to maintain an open and welcoming atmosphere in the learning environment.

Above all, teachers must trust the child in his/her ability to make the appropriate choices for their learning, whilst ensuring that the learning environment is diverse and provides for all the needs of the children in the classroom. In addition, teachers must be of a humble disposition so that they are able to learn from and with the child.

Key points

1 Children's learning in Montessori classrooms is organised in three-year age spans.
2 The organisation of learning is guided by each individual's developmental needs as reflected in their sensitive periods.
3 Children's days consist of three-hour spans, during which they are engaged in a wide variety of activities and have access to both the indoor and outdoor classrooms.
4 Babies and toddlers are given freedom to move and manipulate their environment as they develop their manipulative and language skills and develop positive relationships with practitioners.
5 Children at the nursery age develop their autonomy and demonstrate growing initiative. The focus of their learning is on refinement of the senses and on introduction to literacy and numeracy whilst they grow in their knowledge and understanding of the world.
6 Primary-school-age children need a wider environment for their learning. They develop their mathematical and literacy skills, which are practised and integrated into their study of the Five Great Lessons,
7 To deliver Montessori education across all of these age groups, the teachers need to be knowledgeable about the use of Montessori learning materials.
8 Montessori teachers must be able to give children the opportunity to lead their own learning; they must be prepared to learn with and from children.
9 They must use observation as the key tool for the development of appropriate curricula.
10 The learning environment is an essential component of the Montessori approach; it changes as the children develop and mature.

Reflections

1 Consider the organisation of Montessori classrooms and reflect on it in relation to:
   ■ your own experiences of school
   ■ your current workplace
   ■ adult attitudes to education

2　Identify the fundamental changes which occur in the delivery of Montessori education from one age group to another and consider them in context of:
- your knowledge of children's development
- your own practice
- your partnership with parents

3　Explore the possibility of introducing aspects of Montessori classroom organisation in your setting and consider:
- why and how you would introduce them in your setting
- how you would share these changes with your colleagues
- how you would engage children and their parents in this process of change

4　Reflect on your role in your setting and consider:
- the tasks you do well and why
- the tasks at which you would like to be better and why
- what you could learn from your colleagues

5　Reflect on your relationships with the children in your setting. Do you trust and respect them as equal partners in learning?
- if yes – list three examples for doing so
- if no – explore why you find it difficult
- identify at least two examples of how you could make your relationship with the children more open and balanced

References

Erikson, E.H. (1940) *Childhood and Society*. New York: W.W. Norton.

Lillard, P.P. and Lillard Jessen, L. (2003) *Montessori from the Start*. New York: Schocken Books.

Loeffler, M.H. (ed.) (1992) *Montessori in Contemporary American Culture*. Portsmouth: Heinemann Educational Books, Inc.

MCI (Montessori Centre International) (2010) *Montessori Philosophy, Module 1*. London: MCI.

Montanaro, S.Q. (1991) *Understanding the Human Being*. Mountain View, CA: Nienhuis Montessori USA.

Montessori M. (1965) *The Discovery of the Child*. Cambridge. MA: Robert Bentley Inc.

Montessori, M. (1991) [1918] *The Advanced Montessori Method – Volume 1*. Oxford: ABC – Clio Ltd, Volume 9.

Montessori, M. (2007a) [1949] *The Absorbent Mind*. Amsterdam: Montessori-Pierson Publishing Company, Volume 1.

Montessori, M. (2007b) [1912] *The Discovery of the Child* (originally published as *The Montessori Method*). Amsterdam: Montessori-Pierson Publishing Company, Volume 2.

Montessori, M. (2007e) [1948] *From Childhood to Adolescence*. Amsterdam: Montessori-Pierson Publishing Company, Volume 12.

4 Principles of Montessori pedagogy

This chapter explores the principles of child-initiated education in Montessori settings. It explains the pedagogical tools which facilitate spontaneous learning and teaching strategies employed by Montessori teachers in support of child-led learning.

> The fundamental principle of … pedagogy must be the freedom of the pupil.
> (Montessori 1965: 28)

> There is only one basis for observation: the children must be free to express themselves and thus reveal those needs and attitudes which would otherwise remain hidden or repressed in an environment that did not permit them to act spontaneously. An observer … must have at his disposal children placed in such an environment that they can manifest their natural traits.
> (Montessori 2007a: 48)

Child-centred learning in a Montessori context

Montessori, alongside other educators such as Rousseau (1712–1771), Froebel (1782–1852) and Steiner (1861–1925), placed the child at the centre of the education process. She believed that, to witness children's development unfolding naturally, we need to create environments which will enable the adults 'to follow the child's lead'. Practically, this means that the child's learning focuses on his/her interests whilst the teacher ensures that these interests encompass all aspects of the curriculum. This requires a teacher who:

- understands children's development and the Montessori pedagogy;
- has detailed knowledge of the child's interests and learning styles;
- utilises a wide range of resources.

In all Montessori classrooms observation is the key tool of the teacher's trade and is paramount in ensuring breadth of learning for each child. For Montessori (2007a), learning and development go hand-in-hand, and given adequate freedom with some responsibility, the child's natural aptitudes and interests unfold and should be followed.

Montessori teaching strategies are based on the idea that, given a developmentally appropriate learning environment, children are capable of teaching themselves by selecting activities of interest and investigating them. Montessori (2007a, 2007b) termed this type of learning *self-construction*. Her observation of children led her to the belief that young people are capable of learning in these conditions. She promoted education which guides children in preparation for adult life by becoming knowledgeable and understanding of their environment and who are socially aware individuals ready to defend human rights, the ecology of our planet and, above all, the need for universal peace (Montessori 1992).

The teacher's role in supporting children's learning

Montessori (1991, 2007a, 2007b) recognised that to be able to support the child in his/her self-construction it is essential for the teacher's role and attitudes to change. In her writing, she refers to the teacher as a *director/directress* indicating that the role is to direct the child on the path of self-construction. Such a person requires certain qualities which Montessori (1991, 2007a, 2007b) identified as the ability to stand back from the child and give him/her the opportunity to make choices reflecting his/her interests. The child who benefits from such attitudes grows to be the leader of his/her own learning without the overbearing influence of the teacher. This approach is particularly relevant to the youngest children, whose sense of self-worth is built around their autonomy and growing competence, which is usually the result of opportunities to repeat and perfect skills and activities. This autonomy guides the child towards initiative and the ability to embrace challenge and risk taking – qualities to be encouraged in the children of today, whose personal freedom is often limited.

Montessori (1991, 2007a, 2007b) speaks of the teacher's 'spiritual preparation'. The teacher's ability to reflect on his/her actions and learn from them is part of this preparation. His/her attitudes towards the child need to reflect empathy, personal humility and a genuine wish to serve the child.

All the above characteristics of the teacher's role significantly contribute towards the child's spontaneous learning and development. However, there is another element of the role which Montessori (1991, 2007a, 2007b) writes about and which needs to be considered: the teacher's personal preparation for the role. In today's language the teacher needs to:

- believe in the unique potential of each child and their fundamental 'goodness'. This is in contrast to the Catholic doctrine which was at the heart of Montessori's own upbringing, that of the child being born with Original Sin;
- serve the child in his/her effort of self-construction, which requires belief and trust in the child's capability to learn by him/her self without much adult interference;
- be patient, humble and respectful of the child's efforts by putting aside the desire to control the child;
- be able to reflect on one's own practice and learn from it, using personal experience, dialogue with colleagues and further study of current trends and research as a guide to his/her reflections;
- be an advocate for the child, who heralds the future of humanity and wields potential for social change.

To follow the above principles and considerations, the teacher has at his/her disposal the favourable environment, which includes a range of Montessori learning materials and activities with their unique qualities and characteristics (see Chapter 6). If the teacher understands these fully, they will equip him/her to prepare a wide range of activities to extend the child's learning in support of his/her interests and needs.

Key person

English Montessori nurseries have implemented the key person system in keeping with the requirements of the EYFS (DfE 2017). Their role is to take special responsibility for a group of children, document each child's learning and act as a link between the family, nursery and child. They also 'hold the child in mind' as they ensure their well-being (Manning-Morton and Thorp 2003). The younger the child, the more important the role of the key person is, as she/he becomes the 'voice of the child'. The key person is essential in providing consistency, predictability and availability in relation to the children's everyday life and their relationships with the setting, thereby enabling attachment and positive relationships to grow. This does not mean that the children in the setting only relate to the key person. It is important that a young child develops relationships with all the practitioners in the setting and that all practitioners contribute to the child's observations and records. This provides for a richer picture of the child and draws on a range of expertise of the adults in the setting.

Montessori speaks of the changing role of the teacher, where the child gradually takes over the management of his/her own learning (Standing 1984). For the approach to work effectively, Montessori teachers must understand their role in ensuring that the favourable environment satisfies all the developmental needs and interests of the children in the classroom. The fact that their role seems passive, in the context of traditional education, in no way undermines their significance, contribution or influence over the children's learning.

Key principles of Montessori pedagogy

Before we examine the specific teaching and learning strategies appropriate to the children's age groups, it is important to consider some key principles which underpin classroom management of all Montessori settings and which make a significant contribution to the child's self-construction.

These key principles relate to:

- freedom;
- work-cycle and cycle of activity;
- vertical grouping;
- control of error;
- scaffolding;
- three period lesson;
- observation and assessment;
- promoting self-discipline in Montessori environments.

Freedom in Montessori classrooms

In Montessori classrooms, the children's freedom lies at the heart of their spontaneous learning. This is often the most misunderstood element of

Montessori practice. Some perceive it as a free-for-all, whilst others see the whole approach as too structured, constraining the children's creativity and spontaneous actions. Montessori (1991) saw freedom as an essential component of the child's emerging self-regulation and, as such, it carries social responsibility towards oneself as well as the group, which is appropriate to the age of the children. Thus freedom is limited by the environment. The limitations emerge from, and are embedded in, the class-room environment and are expressed in the form of ground rules. Ground rules ensure the children's safety and well-being. They should be dis-cussed and negotiated with the children. It is important that the ground rules are clearly understood by all and adhered to by everyone in the group, including adults, and that they are consistently applied.

When speaking of children's freedom, consider the freedom of move-ment as directly linked with freedom of choice. It enables the child to move freely around the classroom, choosing activities, selecting where to do them and with whom and for how long. Thus it underpins both the freedom to repeat an activity or not to engage directly with it, as some children learn passively by observing others.

Freedom in Montessori classrooms is facilitated by the organisation of the classroom – the open shelves with materials accessible and ready for use, and by the *work-cycle* and *cycles of activity*. The children's achievements during the work-cycle and cycles of activity can be recorded on a tracking tool which Montessori named the *curve of work*, a graph which documents the activities in which the child engages and their length.

The work-cycle and cycles of activity

As described in Chapter 3 the work-cycle usually spans the morning and is at least two and half hours long, but can stretch across the whole day and is only interrupted by the lunchtime routine. It may also be in place in the afternoons if a new group of children attends the setting. In mainstream nurseries this spontaneous access to activities is referred to as 'continuous provision' (BAECE 2012). During this time children engage in several cycles of activity. Each cycle starts and finishes at the shelf where the activity has its place. The length of the cycle depends on the child's age as well as level of concentration and engagement.

The activities and materials selected during the work-cycle may be done alone, with a friend, in a small group or with one of the teachers. They may take a couple of minutes but can also extend to 30 to 40 minutes if they really engage the child. They may prompt repetitions of the task, usually observed in the behaviours of younger children acquiring new skills and being driven by their need for independence. With older children, one sees that the initial activity often leads towards deeper engagement and critical thinking (BAECE 2012) and so may extend to an hour or longer, and may also lead to engagement with other children or one of the teachers. It may be interrupted by the child's need for a snack, by looking up information in a book or by contemplation. If this is the case, the children make it obvious to everyone else in the group that they wish to return to the task later by placing their name on their work.

The key to the success of the work-cycle is the adults' acknowledgement that children need to be able to make spontaneous choices and that the management of the classroom needs to facilitate these choices. From the teacher's point of view it is important to give the child the choice if they wish to join in an activity. From the child's point of view it is important to recognise that, when they have made a decision to do something, the well-being of the group needs to be considered and the cycle of activity adhered to. Respect for the child's decisions and trust in their ability to make appropriate decisions are paramount aspects of the Montessori approach across all age groups.

Vertical grouping

Chapter 2 considered the importance of grouping children following the three year age spans within the individual stages of development. So effectively children from birth to three learn together, as do three- to six-year-olds, six- to nine-year-olds, nine- to twelve-year-olds and so on. According to Montessori, these groupings are important because they offer children opportunities to learn as a 'family' or 'community', and thus reflect a more natural organisation of children's learning. This approach also enhances children's cooperation; it provides the older ones with an opportunity to guide the younger children and so consolidate their understanding as they share their knowledge with their younger or less able peers. Examining this approach from the perspective of the children receiving help, learning from friends is more accessible and often more enjoyable, as most children admire and look up to their more able peers.

Vertical grouping underpins developing social relationships and emotional well-being, whereby children are able to display sympathy, empathy and concern for each other while demonstrating their emotional intelligence. Montessori practitioners find this is one of the elements of Montessori pedagogy which is particularly difficult to maintain, as pressure from the educational establishment as well as parents seriously undermines this tool for social cohesion, despite its effective scaffolding of children's learning (Montessori 2007a). Once children reach kindergarten age (five and six years old) and compulsory school age, they are usually organised in groups determined by their age, as this is perceived by conventional education as more suited to teaching techniques and strategies and assessment. Montessori practitioners believe that grouping by age can promote unhealthy competition amongst children and parents and often hinders the efforts of the less able children.

Control of error

Montessori (2007a, 2007b) refers in her writing to the autodidactic (self-teaching) nature of the Montessori favourable environment and the materials within it. Each activity or set of materials has a clearly defined purpose. The child engaging with it should benefit, particularly from the cognitive perspective and from growing manipulative skills. Language and social skills are also considered, as is the undisputed emotional benefit of the child's growing independence as their competence expands. Whatever the child chooses to do in the favourable environment should promote learning and development because the teacher only includes activities and materials they believe benefit the children. In addition to the strong focus on identified outcomes, Montessori also built into some of the activities a device which helps the child to problem solve and find an appropriate solution to a given challenge. She refers to it as the *control of error* (Montessori 2007b). Control of error relates particularly to activities with one-to-one correspondence, for example puzzles or knobbed cylinders – specific Montessori materials for the younger children which call upon the child's problem-solving skills of trial and error.

For the older child, Montessori devised a control of error that provides tools for checking one's work with the help of control cards which give the correct answers. Both types of control of error are designed to minimise the child's dependence on adult help and contribute to the child's self-construction.

Sometimes so-called 'control of error' devices are added by practitioners to complement the existing materials. One example involves placing matching colour dots or numbers on objects designed to be matched and paired, such as sound cylinders, which are part of the activities for refinement of the senses. These devices certainly add another point of interest to the activity, but do not actually provide an effective control of error

Presentation tray

because children quickly work out that they can match the cylinders by turning them upside down and matching the colour dots or numbers rather than carefully listening to the sounds of each cylinder and finding the corresponding pair.

Control of error is often misunderstood. The fact that Montessori referred to her materials as autodidactic does not automatically mean that all the activities have a built-in control of error. Another aspect to consider is the fact that children need to be able to perceive the error in order to control it (Morris-Coole 2007). Practitioners do not always know or understand fully what engages children, particularly the younger ones. Often it is the sensory quality of the materials which attracts them rather than the predetermined benefit of a specific piece of material; in such circumstances the engagement with the activity is also of benefit to the child's development.

Scaffolding children's learning

Another unique feature of Montessori activities lies in their careful design and progression in learning, which enables children to learn a new skill or concept via 'scaffolding'. That is, each activity focuses on a unique quality within the activity, building up the child's knowledge and skill in small, manageable steps whilst they grow in competence and understanding. Children are encouraged to repeat the activities until they master a specific skill or demonstrate understanding of a specific concept. This strategy applies to all areas of learning.

The following examples demonstrate scaffolding in action.

Using scissors

Most young children love to use scissors, so mastering the skill of cutting can be an exciting challenge. Recognising that using toy scissors, which do not cut, is frustrating and counterproductive practitioners harness the child's interest whilst showing them how to use real scissors safely. They start by ensuring that alongside the scissors, which are available to the children on the shelf, there are also small trays on which they can be carried. Also available are strips of paper narrower than the blades of the scissors, initially enabling the child to make the cut with one snip of the scissors. First they practise how to hold the scissors, then they work on opening and closing the blades; next they place the blades at a right angle to the strip of paper and close them to make a cut whilst holding the strip of paper with the other hand. Knowing where and how to hold the strip is a real skill in itself and needs to be practised as much as the use of the scissors. When this skill is mastered, the next strip, of the same width, has lines drawn across to focus the child's attention on where to place the blades before cutting along the line. When this skill is mastered, strips with more complex lines such as zigzags or curves are introduced, allowing the child to gradually develop control of the scissors by making several cuts, one after the other along the line, without removing the scissors from the paper. This preparation gives children skills to follow a specific outline, accurately cutting pictures out of postcards or making an intricate paper cutting. It may take several months to perfect these cutting skills. Each step engages the child because it is manageable and achievable, yet provides sufficient new challenge to move the child along in their learning.

Colour boxes

Another example, the use of the three colour boxes (Chapter 6) designed by Montessori to help children refine their chromatic sense, effectively demonstrates the scaffolding of children's understanding of colours in the environment.

Colour box 1, containing just three pairs of tablets in primary colours – red, blue and yellow – is usually introduced to children early on, once they have expressed an interest in colours. Children learn how to hold the tablets, how to take them out of their box and how to match and pair them. They are also introduced to the names of colours, which is accomplished by using the three-period lesson discussed later in this chapter. They are also encouraged to take each tablet and find objects of matching colours in the environment, both inside and outside, thus demonstrating their knowledge and understanding of the application of the colour.

If they enjoy Colour box 1 and are competent in its use, they are then introduced to Colour box 2, which contains eleven pairs of tablets – the original primary colours, the secondary colours (green, purple, orange), white and black as well as pink, grey and brown. Once again the tablets are matched and paired, objects of corresponding colours can be found in the environment and names introduced. Previously learned skills scaffold newly emerging ones. For instance, the child may explore how secondary colours are made, either accidentally whilst painting or in organised lessons using food colouring or paints on wet paper. Secondary colours of light can also be explored using plastic colour disks. This should lead to the

Cutting samples

discovery that secondary colours made with light are different to those made with paints. All the time the child also explores colours in the surroundings of the setting, particularly in the natural environment. This may lead to further exploration of colour and light by creating a rainbow with the help of a prism, or talking about the rainbow after having seen it during a rain shower.

When the children's knowledge and understanding of colours is well established, the setting can introduce Colour box 3, which contains the nine colours children know from Colour box 2, each in seven new shades. This gives the opportunity to organise the tablets in sequence from light to dark or vice versa, using observational skills to identify small differences in each tablet. Usually, by the time children are ready for this activity they are also ready to play collaboratively with their friends, and may decide to grade all 63 tablets either in rows or in a spectacular colour wheel, taking a good 40 to 50 minutes in organising all the tablets. This example gives a rich picture of how the child's knowledge and understanding of colour is scaffolded in Montessori settings over a period of time, supported by specific Montessori materials and other activities readily available in the classroom.

Colour wheel

Social awareness and consideration for others

The fact that in the nursery catering for three- to six-year-olds there is usually just one of each activity or one set of materials scaffolds children's social awareness and ability to wait for their turn. Children learn quickly that when they take an activity from the shelf they will be given the opportunity to engage with it for as long as they wish, provided they return it to the shelf ready for another child to use. This approach also gives them an opportunity to invite a friend to join in or work on one's own. The clearly defined routine of cycles of activity makes a significant contribution to classroom management and children's growing social awareness. They are often reminded by their peers or the adults in the classroom to put their activity back on the shelf so that it is ready for another child to use.

Indirect preparation for later learning

Many of the activities undertaken when first in the nursery support the more academic learning which follows. Montessori (2007b) speaks of children receiving indirect preparation for later learning. This is another example of children's learning being scaffolded and progression in learning encouraged. For example, the sorting, matching and pairing activities within the sensorial area support the children's ability to organise and classify information and so underpin their logical thinking, as well as prepare them for later learning in numeracy and understanding the world areas. Another example of such preparation is the exploration of texture, particularly sandpaper in the sensorial area, which prepares the child for use of the sandpaper letters, numerals and the globe.

Developing manipulative skills

The many activities which develop the child's manipulative skills, such as cutting, sewing and pegging, strengthen the fingers and promote dexterity and flexibility of the wrist, contributing positively towards the child's developing writing skills. Single skills introduced in the area of everyday living such as pouring, cutting, wiping of surfaces or washing of dishes after a snack are combined in more complex activities such as cooking, which draws upon all of these skills.

Colour coding

Another example of scaffolding and helping the child in the organisation of information is colour coding, particularly in literacy. Colour coding can be applied to the identification of vowels (blue) and consonants (red) in the Large Moveable Alphabet, which enables children to build words before they have the physical skills of forming letters (see Chapter 6).

Colour coding is also used in the identification of parts of speech where each element is represented by a specific colour and individual words are written on the specific colour card, for example: nouns on black or verbs on red. This enables the child to form sentences using words written on the coloured card, so that a pattern of sentence formation emerges.

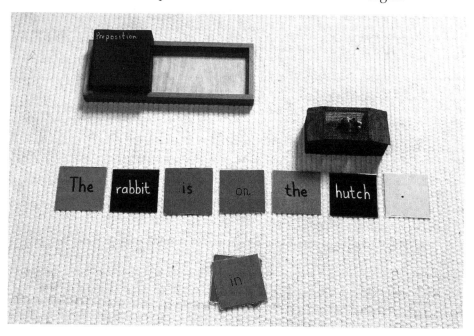

Colour-coded sentence

In addition, colour coding is used in arithmetic to identify the hierarchies of the decimal system with units – a unit of thousands represented by green numerals, tens and tens of thousands written in blue and hundreds and hundreds of thousands in red.

Extensive use of colour coding is made in geography and biology, where continents are identified by specific colours – for example green for Africa and pink for South America – and the phyla of the animal kingdom are presented to the child on coloured cards (deep blue for all

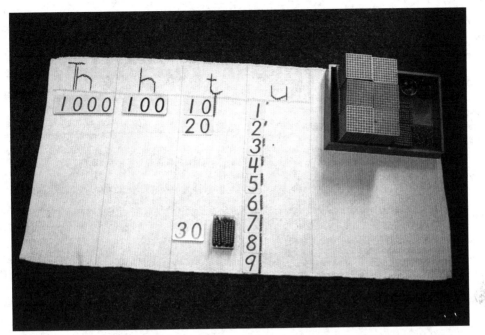

Counting with golden beads – working with the decimal system

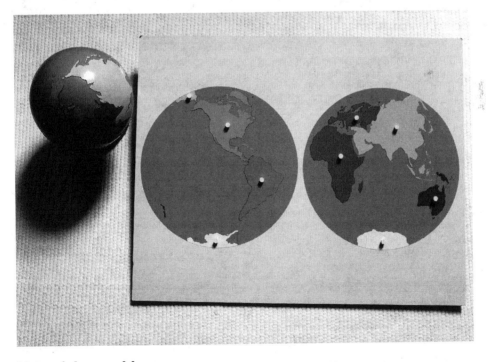

Map of the world

chordates), which are further subdivided into the five classes of: fish (light green), amphibians (purple), reptiles (brown), birds (light blue) and mammals (red). From early contact with the images of these animals, the colour indirectly suggests to the child that all animals presented on red cards belong together and have some common features, which are later explained.

The three-period lesson – extending children's vocabulary

Montessori recognised the importance of the adult when supporting children's language development, particularly so during the sensitive period for language. She advocated exposing babies and toddlers to every-day language (Montessori 2007a); she wanted them to be part of a family and community, participating in shopping expeditions, preparing and eating family meals, and fully integrating into everyday life. She believed that this type of engagement could give young children an opportunity to absorb the language of the home and support their language acquisition (Montessori 1966, 2007a). She also adopted Seguin's three-period lesson for the teaching of new vocabulary, especially new names of objects in the environment. This lesson has become one of the key teaching tools of the Montessori approach and is particularly useful for helping children learn names of specific utensils, plants and animals, as well as the sensorial materials or their qualities, such as colours and textures. It is often referred to as the naming game. The game gives a child the opportunity to associate a new name with a particular object. As the name suggests, it is a lesson in three parts:

1 At first an object (such as the blue colour tablet) is placed in front of a child and named several times. It is then replaced by another assoc-iated object (the red colour tablet), which is again named several times. Often a third object is introduced in the same way (the yellow colour tablet). This may be repeated again to reinforce the new name. For example, the teacher may say, 'This is blue, blue, blue', pointing to the blue tablet.

2 In the second stage, two or three objects (such as the three colour tablets from Colour box 1) are placed in front of the child and the game continues with the teacher asking the child to point to a named object, to feel it or to move it. For example, the teacher asks, 'Can you show me the blue/the red/the yellow?' The child identifies each colour as it is named.

3   In the third stage, all the objects are placed in front of the child once again and the child is asked to name an identified object. For example, the teacher points to the blue tablet and says, 'What colour is this?'

It is not necessary to present all three stages during the same lesson. Often the game finishes at the end of the second stage, and the next day it starts with the second stage and follows onto the final one. Montessori practitioners also use the three-period lesson when introducing children to the sandpaper letters and teaching them to count.

In terms of the child's learning, during the three-period lesson the object is at first isolated and named, then the name is reinforced by hearing it again and selecting the appropriate object, whereas at the last stage the child may be able to name the object. Observing siblings or friends together, one occasionally witnesses exactly the same process when one of them teaches a new name to the other child. It is a particularly useful tool when working with newcomers to the setting, when the language of the setting may be different to the child's home language.

Observations and assessment of children's learning

Despite the fact that Montessori was one of the first pedagogues to use observation as an effective tool for getting to know children, she left behind little documentation on observational methodology apart from the *curve of work* (Montessori 1991). However, observations remain the key tool for assessment of learning of young children. In Montessori settings observations are undertaken daily using a variety of methods. These range from brief jottings of children's achievements, sayings or interests to dated entries in a checklist such as the Individual Learning Plan (ILP) used by many Montessori nurseries. The ILP documents children's progression of learning in a list of activities available in the setting organised according to Montessori areas of learning. It is a quick way of tracking children's progress in a range of activities on offer and also helps to guide planning of activities, as the plan lists the intended progression of activities. This ILP has been used by several companies to develop a digital recording system which helps to track the children's progress along the developmental lines leading towards achievement of the EYFS early learning goals (DfE 2017).

Montessori teachers also make longer narrative observations which provide a deeper insight into the child's levels of engagement with the materials, their problem-solving and thinking, language and manipulative skills as well as responses to friends, peers and adults in the nursery during play. The observations are often supported with photographs and samples of children's work. All this documentation provides evidence for the child's formative assessment and underpins the end-of-term or end-of-year report, a summative record of the child's progress.

The formative assessment supports other record-keeping systems which may be in place, such as the EYFS Profile. Montessori recognised early on that formal tests are not beneficial to the children's learning and development at any age. Her main focus was on the levels of concentration and engagement in activities which children chose to do. For this purpose, she used the *curve of work* (Montessori 1991). Today's Montessori teachers often combine the *curve of work* with the Leuven Scale of Engagement (Laevers 1994) to measure not only the length of engagement but also the level, and to document the child's well-being. When combined together, these tools provide some interesting data regarding individual children's levels of engagement and concentration in relation to selected activities undertaken during any *work-cycle*. The focus on levels of engagement can be also related to the characteristics of effective learning as outlined in the EYFS (DfE 2012), which will be discussed in more detail in Chapter 5.

Montessori saw the main focus of her education system as the child's self-construction leading to a well-informed, sensitive and aware adult – who enjoys learning and life. These adults actively participate in their community and advocate harmonious, respectful relationships within their community and in their environment. In the Montessori approach to education children are helped to enjoy learning and see it as a lifelong journey, developing into strong individuals who are able to make decisions for and by themselves, and to have a deep understanding of their social responsibility. These characteristics are fostered by helping children develop their self-worth, self-awareness and self-discipline.

Promoting self-discipline in Montessori environments

According to Montessori, 'an individual is disciplined when he is master of himself and he can, as a consequence, control himself when he must follow the rule of life' (2007b: 51). For Montessori (2007a), obedience and self-discipline go hand-in-hand with an environment which offers children freedom within limits and with responsibility appropriate to their development and maturity. The key lies in positive role modelling and in opportunities to engage in self-chosen activities. This freedom fulfils the inner needs of the child and promotes concentration and deep engagement, which are essential to emerging self-regulation.

The freedom in Montessori nurseries is linked with responsibilities, such as having to return activities back on the shelves so they can be used by another child. These responsibilities are linked with the ground rules of the classroom which are designed to promote social awareness. Responsibility is fostered by encouraging children's independence. It is nurtured from the early days in Montessori settings and becomes the foundation of the self-discipline witnessed in children who benefit from Montessori education. The emerging self-discipline is closely linked with the children's developmental stage and maturity.

Initially, children learn to control their movements. Their growing competence and independence, as well as the dawning of the ability to control their impulses, all contribute to the emerging social individual who is beginning to be aware not only of his or her needs, but also the needs and well-being of others within the group and its social conventions. According to Montessori (1991), this child is ready for primary education.

In primary school, self-discipline is evident in the child's ability to contribute to and follow a learning plan for a day, and later for a whole week. The child's freedom to concentrate on tasks according to his/her own rhythms, wishes and cohort of friends carries the responsibility of ensuring the tasks are completed to the best of the child's ability and within the agreed timeframe.

The sensitive period for moral development is evident in the children's concern for other, less fortunate peers. Children of this age often organise fundraising events during various disasters such as the Syrian child refugees or the Grenfell Tower disaster of recent years. These events give children the opportunity to contribute either by doing something to fundraise or by donating their pocket money, books and toys. Adults are often moved by the children's selfless generosity. These are instances of children's ability to defer gratification for the benefit of others, an important element of self-regulation.

Children who have learned to organise their education and social life, and who understand that they have a responsibility to themselves as well as to those in their group and community, are truly children ready to enter the turbulent teenage years. It is the author's belief that these children find adolescence less challenging.

Key points

1 The Montessori approach conceives of the child as the leader of learning.
2 Montessori teachers are facilitators of children's learning. By preparing the learning environment, they ensure that children are provided with tools for all aspects of their development.
3 Assessments in Montessori classrooms are based on observations, which also serve as tools for planning. Levels of engagement and concentration are the barometers of children's successful learning.
4 Activities and learning are developmentally appropriate and reflect the children's sensitive periods.
5 Children's learning is characterised by freedom with responsibility. The responsibility is defined by the environment itself and by the ground rules which promote social awareness.
6 Children are grouped vertically in spans of three years.
7 Learning is organised into *work-cycles* and *cycles of activity* which support children's personal rhythms, spontaneous learning and guide them in developing responsibility for their actions.
8 Montessori learning materials promote auto-education, and some of them have a built-in control of error. Children's learning is scaffolded by the design of activities. Their learning is also aided by colour coding.
9 Children's vocabulary is developed by the use of the three-period lesson.
10 The success of Montessori teaching lies in the fostering of self-worth, self-awareness and self-discipline, so contributing towards the emergence of responsible adults.

Reflections

1 Consider the approach you have to working with children and what (and why) it is important to you as an educator. Reflect on children's:
   ■ knowledge and understanding of the topic identified in the curriculum
   ■ opportunities and ability to express their understanding of the topic
   ■ preparation for examinations

2 Consider how the *work-cycle* would fit into your setting:
   ■ what are the advantages/disadvantages of whole group work?

- what could be the implications of introducing a snack when children are not ready?
- would you trust the children in your class to manage their own learning?

3   Consider your own teaching strategies:
- could you introduce the control of error?
- how could you incorporate colour coding into teaching?
- would you consider introducing vertical grouping and why?

4   How do you scaffold children's learning?
- how and why do you set children targets?
- what is your view on integrating learning across all areas of the curriculum within a lesson?
- what benefits do you see in peer learning?

5   Explore the idea of nurturing the individual:
- why and how would you promote self-awareness and self-worth as essential components of well-being?
- consider the benefits of tests and examinations for the child, the parents and the school
- which elements of your own practice promote self-discipline in children?

References

BAECE (British Association of Early Childhood Education) (2012) *Development Matters*. London: BAECE.

DfE (Department for Education) (2012) *Statutory Framework for Early Years Foundation Stage*. London: DfE.

DfE (2017) *The Early Years Foundation Stage Framework*. London: DfE. Online: www.gov.uk/government/uploads/system/uploads/attachment_data/file/596629/EYFS_STATUTORY_FRAMEWORK_2017.pdf

Laevers, F. (ed.) (1994) *Defining and Assessing Quality in Early Childhood Education*. Leuven, Belgium: Leuven University Press.

Manning-Morton, J. and Thorp, M. (2003) *Key Times for Play*. Maidenhead: Open University Press.

Montessori, M. (1965) [1914] *Dr Montessori's Own Handbook*. New York: Schocken Books.

Montessori M. (1966) *The Secret of Childhood*. Notre Dame, IL: Fides Publishers.

Montessori, M. (1991) [1918] *The Advanced Montessori Method – Volume 1*. Oxford: ABC – Clio Ltd.

Montessori, M. (1992) [1949] *Education and Peace*. Oxford: ABC – Clio Ltd, Volume 10.

Montessori, M. (2007a) [1949] *The Absorbent Mind*. Amsterdam: Montessori-Pierson Publishing Company, Volume 1.

Montessori, M. (2007b) [1912] *The Discovery of the Child* (originally published as *The Montessori Method*). Amsterdam: Montessori-Pierson Publishing Company, Volume 2.

Morris-Coole, S (2007) *The Control of Error*. Montessori International, October–December.

Standing, E.M. (1984) *Maria Montessori, Her Life and Work*. New York: Plume.

5 Learning in Montessori settings

This chapter explains how and what children are learning in Montessori settings from birth to the age of twelve with a focus on early childhood. It makes links with the Early Years Foundation Stage (EYFS) and outlines how children's learning is shared with parents. The characteristics of effective learning are explained in the context of Montessori practice.

> When there is motor and physical activity, you can see a more important kind of education, a kind of education that takes the force of life into account.
>
> (Montessori 2012: 65)

> The instructions of a teacher consist merely of a hint, a touch – enough to give a start to the child.
>
> (Montessori 1965: 58–59)

Learning across the age groups

As identified in previous chapters, children's learning reflects their developmental stages, maturity and interests. These elements are mirrored in the activities on offer in the classroom, in the organisation of the class-room and in the length of the *work-cycle*. The focus is on individual learning and development, particularly in the first six years of life. It is unusual for young children to be expected to participate in whole class lessons or circle times attended by all the children. The principle of freedom of choice is firmly rooted in all activities. Therefore children tend to have a snack when they are ready for it, rather than as part of a group. Small groups participating in singing, story time or a talk about a specific topic evolve naturally, initiated by a teacher or a child, with others joining if they wish. In primary schools, friends often negotiate and plan on doing activities relating to the Great Lessons together. They benefit from brainstorming, discussions and debates which may involve either a small group or the whole class. They learn about democratic decision making and are deeply concerned about being fair and just.

Montessori practice and the Early Years Foundation Stage

The principles which underpin the delivery of the EYFS are powerful statements which are aligned with the key principles of all early years pioneers – Wilhelm Froebel, Rudolf Steiner, the Macmillan sisters, Susan Isaacs and also Maria Montessori. They all advocate focus on individual children and the need to nurture their uniqueness by fostering meaningful relationship with peers and adults and to establish rich learning environments both inside and outside the classroom. When practitioners have a shared understanding of these principles then learning and development are guided by them irrespective of the teaching approaches adopted by the individual pedagogies.

From the Montessori perspective, each child has always been and continues to be at the heart of the learning process. Each individual is celebrated as unique and is supported by knowledgeable and sensitive adults who work with parents and the wider community to ensure that the favourable environment provides all that the child needs to develop and follow a natural path of development. It is the purpose of Chapters 4, 5 and 6 to explain how learning and development unfold and are managed.

Learning in the infant community

The focus of learning at this age is on giving babies and toddlers opportunities to move and use all parts of their bodies to develop gross motor skills and coordination of movement both inside and outside, and to begin refining their fine motor and manipulative skills. The children learn through their senses, by exploring everyday and new objects in their environment, absorbing the objects' properties such as texture, weight, smell, colour and shape and assigning names to them. Children begin to gain independence in personal hygiene, dressing and putting on their shoes and feeding themselves. Their understanding of how their home and nursery environment work grows rapidly, as does their vocabulary and ability to move and manipulate objects. In a well-prepared classroom, the learning is spontaneous, with planning guided by the children's sensitive periods.

Gradually the children learn how freedom of choice works and are able to decide what they want to do. Often, they will engage with an activity where it is displayed on the shelf, standing whilst they are doing it. For this reason the activities on display are few and are rotated regularly. There are also several activities offered which are very similar in order to avoid conflict over their use, bearing in mind the egocentric nature of the child at this age.

As discussed in Chapter 6, heuristic play is part and parcel of many Montessori infant communities (Goldschmied and Jackson 2004). It supports the children's sensitive periods by providing predictability and consistency in the way activities are offered to children, thus nurturing their sensitivity to order. Treasure baskets also offer opportunities for sensory exploration and encourage sustained periods of concentration whilst the child learns to make choices. Often, the treasure baskets are modified for older children and serve as tools for developing vocabulary as well as encouraging grouping of objects with their photographs.

Toddlers also have access to heuristic bags, which supports their deep desire to move and carry things. These bags contain a variety of objects which can be sorted, posted and fitted inside each other – this enables learning about relationships and size, as well as other properties of objects. Toddlers demonstrate their sensitive period for detail in spotting small differences in books, their favourite bugs in the garden and the environment. First-hand experience provides rich sensory learning for the children of this age, particularly when these are available both in the classroom and outside – in the garden and in local parks and the community. They notice and possibly get upset if their friends and adults are missing from the classroom.

Their language skills become extended through learning songs and rhymes, daily story telling and book reading, moving to music and dancing. Daily visits to the nursery garden and walks in local parks further contribute to their learning.

The main focus of learning in this age group is to support the children's sensitive periods for order, movement and language and nurture their independence. Daily routines of dressing, eating and toileting contribute significantly to the children's growing autonomy and support their emerging sense of self. The focus is on the child's well-being – physical, intellectual and emotional. These key sensitive periods of the spiritual embryonic stage (Montessori 2007a) are in line with the EYFS prime areas of learning (DfE 2017) and promote the children's personal, social and emotional and physical development and communication and language.

All Montessori settings in England use the two-year check (DfE 2017) as the first assessment of the child on entering the nursery. It is prepared by the child's key person, together with his/her family. Current early years practice recognises the important role of the key person as an essential link between the child, the family and the setting. At this age the key person is an important attachment figure for children attending day nurseries and childminders. She/he facilitates opportunities to secure attachment for the child, thus contributing effectively towards the child's internal working model (Bowlby 1969).

Learning in the children's house

The focus on learning through the senses and manipulation continues. The three- to six-year-olds have access to activities displayed on open shelves and will be able to take full advantage of the freedom to choose whilst following cycles of activity. The activities of everyday living facilitate opportunities for growth in competence whilst using everyday objects such as a range of spoons, ladles, tongs and tweezers, tools essential in arts and crafts and gardening. Children learn culturally appropriate etiquette for setting tables, welcoming visitors and asking for help. They extend their personal independence by brushing their teeth after meals, learning to tie their shoelaces as well as doing up their anorak zips or buttons on coats and jackets.

Their rich sensorial experiences develop further with the help of the sensorial materials. New concepts and conceptual frameworks will be established, all contributing to the child's deeper understanding of the environment as well as the ability to organise and classify information. The materials also serve as preparation for more academic learning when literacy and numeracy are introduced to those children who express an interest in it.

Many seeds of interest and knowledge are sown by introducing children to the creatures living in their garden, to the lifecycle of animals and plants and to the variety of animal life found in their own environment and around the world. As children explore the solar system or the eruption of a volcano, they will learn about their planet and its unique physical features such as rivers and lakes. They will be introduced to the continents of the world and their peoples, cultures and lifestyles as well as animals, plants and transport. The children will learn about the properties of water and basic principles of magnetism and light as they are introduced to floating and sinking, the three states of water and other science phenomena.

All of these activities prepare children for an introduction to phonics and arithmetic when they express an interest as evidenced by the teacher's observation, which usually happens during their time at nursery. The strong foundations laid in the early stages lead them to success in learning at the next stage, having gained competence and self-assurance in the skills and activities they enjoyed, as well as having grown in their social skills.

The social aspects of nursery life are very strong. Each child's unique development is taken into consideration and s/he is guided towards social life both by example and also by providing etiquette and structure during the sharing of activities. Children are asked if they are ready to share with others and their wishes are respected. There are no expectations that, just because a child attends a nursery, they should be ready to share with others. Montessori teachers trust in the natural unfolding of social skills, friendships and empathy as the children settle in, gradually decentre and develop theory of mind (Piaget, in Bruce 2015). All these aspects of learning foster children's well-being. The gradual emergence of initiative and self-discipline is the hallmark of a successful Montessori nursery education.

In the context of the EYFS (DfE 2017) the prime areas of learning continue to be the focus of Montessori nursery education as children refine their physical skills and continue to develop their fine and gross motor skills in the area of everyday living and also in the outdoor classroom by learning to garden, cook and use a variety of utensils. Alongside these activities they will develop their communication and language skills whilst choosing books in the book area, working in the creative area alongside friends and problem solving in the sensorial area of the classroom using Montessori and other activities, such as the unit block. These activities also provide valuable preparation for early numeracy and literacy. Role play provides rich opportunities for children of this age to extent their language and social skills whilst negotiating their play and explaining a variety of role-play scenarios. The knowledge of the world area often includes a nature table which provides a focus for project work reflecting the children's interests.

The Montessori early years curriculum provides a structured intro-duction to mathematics as well as literacy very much in line with the requirements of the EYFS. However, it is important to note that as most children in England leave Montessori settings soon after their fourth birthday their opportunities to benefit from activities in these two areas of learning are limited by their early departure. It is usual for most children to express interest in letters and numbers around the age of three and half and later; therefore three-year-olds attending Montessori settings may be introduced to letter sounds and shapes and start building short words using knowledge of phonics and some will be able to write their names. Unfortunately they will not benefit from the full range of literacy and early grammar activities on offer. Equally the full range of activities to develop their mathematical skills will be limited to counting to twenty and introduction to addition and subtraction.

Much of the work started at nursery will be continued in the child's reception class. The activities on offer will have a stronger focus on literacy and numeracy and learning will be delivered in a more formal manner, however still within the context of a play-based curriculum as the EYFS spans from the age of two all the way to the summer term of the reception year.

Learning in the primary school

The children who experienced Montessori nursery education and progress onto Montessori primary school are fortunate, since the transition from one to the other should be smooth. They bring with them a basic under-standing of freedom with responsibility, and they are able to embrace the parameters of the freedom offered by the primary classroom. They thrive on the responsibility given to them when managing their daily or weekly learning according to their individual plan, combining growing skills in mathematics, reading and writing with research into the Great Lessons following Montessori's ethos of cosmic education.

The Great Lessons give an evolutionary perspective on the development of our planet and its civilisations, starting with the creation of the solar system and evolution of life. The evolution of the human species is the focus of the second Great Story, with progression onto the study of the early civili-sations. The history of writing and mathematics are the topics of the fourth and fifth Great Lessons and give opportunities to explore the great art works and technical and scientific discoveries made by human beings.

The study of the Five Great Lessons can also be approached by focusing on underlying themes, such as water. It is studied in all its aspects – in its liquid, solid and gas states, as the water cycle and as one of the most significant elements changing the nature of our planet from prehistoric times onward. Aspects of physical geography reflect the importance of water on Earth when studying oceans, rivers, lakes and deserts. Water is further linked with the first settlements and early agriculture, and with the history of early civilisations which evolved around the great rivers in all the continents of the Earth. Relevant music, poetry and art are also linked with the topic.

The children's sensitive periods continue to be nurtured by giving them opportunities to study in their wider community and use the resources within it, and by encouraging them to participate in team activities. They develop their sense of right and wrong as their moral awareness and empathy grow. They emerge as strong individuals ready to embrace challenges and offer help to others. Montessori primary schools in England are not required to deliver the National Curriculum however most of them have mapped their Montessori primary curriculum against the National Curriculum to demonstrate the range and scope of the work the children attending their schools experience.

Learning in secondary school

At the time of writing there is only one Montessori secondary school in England, The Montessori Place, established in 2016 in Sussex. The school is based on Montessori's ideal of combining learning with practical experiences of farming and crafts.

Characteristics of early learning and learning in Montessori nurseries

In this section the learning of young children is explained in the context of the EYFS; therefore it is natural that the characteristics of early learning should be explored. These characteristics outline how children are guided towards critical thinking and creativity – important goals of human development. Montessori identifies two key factors which are unique to all human beings – intelligence and imagination:

activity … allows the child to construct intelligence from his experiences … Imagination enables us to acquire our culture, to retain the images that we gather in our minds and to construct with these images … It enables us to see that which is not there.

(Montessori 2012: 173)

By understanding the characteristics of early learning, educators promote the children's capacity to develop a wide range of skills which lay the foundation for the child's emerging imagination. When examining the characteristics of effective learning in a Montessori context we refer to the staged process of effective learning as described in *Development Matters* (BAECE 2012):

- Playing and exploring – engagement
  - Finding out and exploring
  - Playing with what they know
  - Being willing to 'have a go'

- Active learning – motivation
  - Being involved and concentrating
  - Keeping trying
  - Enjoying achieving what they set out to do

- Creating and thinking critically – thinking
  - Having their own ideas
  - Making links
  - Choosing ways to do things

From the Montessori perspective we would say that the children's capacity to learn spontaneously is guided by their inner motivation to do, to engage and get involved.

The favourable environment enables them to find an activity of interest on the open shelves and explore it. They will be given time and space to explore the activity because:

- it is familiar to them, such as pouring from one jug to another or building a tower, painting at an easel, looking at a book or putting a dolly to bed;
- they are curious about it – it has captured their interest;
- maybe their friend is playing with it and they are keen to join.

In all these scenarios they will be willing to have a go because of the key principles of the environment – the child's freedom of choice and movement. It is precisely this freedom to choose that will nurture the next three characteristics of effective learning. The fact that the child has chosen the activity will make him/her motivated to get involved and to concentrate on the activity, and to persevere and enjoy making a necklace, washing the dishes, sweeping the playground, building the pink tower, reading a book or painting a picture.

The children may repeat many of these activities many times before the moment of creativity and creative thinking emerges – the moment when the child has an opportunity to express his/her own ideas, make links and chose his/her own ways of doing things. At this point the child demonstrates to the adult his/her creative impulses or intentions, offering the practitioner an insight into the child's way of thinking. The following scenarios offer some examples of opportunities for the adults to observe and note children's interest:

- Making a necklace may lead the child to:
    - exploration of the sound of the beads as they fall on different surfaces and provide the practitioner with a critical insight that the child is interested in sounds;
    - giving the necklace to a friend or a teacher or a doll – demonstrates the child's need to connect with others.

Thus the child's creativity will take him/her to a new sphere of learning from manipulative skills to social interactions or sensory experiences or maybe both.

- Washing of dishes after snack often demonstrates:
    - deep interest in water and its properties.

- Sweeping of floors may lead us:
    - to pattern making;
    - use of large arm movements using ribbons and dancing;
    - painting with water using large brushes.

- Building the pink tower is often the initial step towards:
    - creation of castles or launch pads;
    - complex abodes for dinosaurs;
    - exploration of monuments and interesting buildings in books and online.

Just consider the observation below and ponder the creative journey from the mud kitchen to the memories from a visit to the Natural History Museum. Children's creativity and thinking takes them and us on unexpected journeys far beyond the adults' wildest imagination.

In a recent observation of the nursery mud kitchen Omar (3.2) is happily exploring the texture of the mud and diligently filling the nearby bucket. He is approached by Thomas (4.5) who throws a plastic fish into the bucket and shouts 'Fish pie'.

Omar is stunned by the interruption, however, Thomas is happy to add other items like small stones, leaves and some pasta into the bucket making sure the fish pie is tasty. They start talking about the food they like and come to realise they both enjoy tuna sandwiches. Omar asks 'What kind of fish is it? Is it like the one you put into the pie?'. The practitioner who was supporting the children in their play in the outside classroom hears this comment and takes this opportunity to chip into the conversation – 'Shall we see if we can find it on the iPad?'. They find pictures of blue-fin tuna and discover they are silvery and large and very sleek and very different to the pinky bits of fish they have in their sandwiches. They see a picture of the biggest tuna ever caught, weighing 411kg, caught by a women off the coast of New Zealand. They start exploring how big 411kg is – what would it take to make a sandpit weighting 411kg and where is New Zealand on the map of the world? After lunch the boys are still thinking about this enormous tuna fish and start putting together pieces of paper to make a model using silver foil to make it shiny – they cut little spikes near the tail – just like they saw on the iPad. These ideas are emerging spontaneously as they are inspired by the plentiful resources in the art area. The finished fish is several metres long and Thomas asks for it to be hung up from the ceiling just like the blue whale he saw when he visited the museum with his parents in the holidays.

In facilitating the 'creating and critical thinking' *the role of the Montessori teacher* is crucial. She or he:

- prepares and maintains the favourable environment;
- ensures that the child has the freedom to move, to choose, not to be interrupted and have the opportunities to repeat and express his/her ideas verbally and through gesture and action;
- observes the process of learning and stands back to enable the child to express him/herself fully;
- observes and then 'seeds' (Siraj Blatchford and Brock 2016) and extends and shares the moment of thinking with the child;

- is respectful and sensitive of the child's efforts;
- gives each child an opportunity for this high level of thinking and expression.

The teacher's capacity to identify moments of 'creating and thinking critically' provides opportunities for seeding of further learning and facilitates new opportunities for the child's creativity to flow and develop further. These opportunities may and often should go beyond what the Montessori classroom offers. They should embrace all aspects of learning. The Montessori activities provide the starting point, the foundation for the exploration and involvement. They are a springboard for the child's growing needs and capabilities and therefore are likely to challenge the adults, giving them numerous opportunities for learning from the child. If such opportunities are created for the child, sustained shared thinking (Sylva et al. 2004) will be in evidence.

Partnership with parents

Montessori was aware of the importance of parent–child relationships. When writing about the unfolding of the sensitive periods in the child's development, she highlighted the role parents and carers can play in supporting the child's optimum maturation. For example, she advocated that babies and toddlers should participate in the everyday life of the family and engage in shopping expeditions, family meals and outings. She believed that very young children absorb all aspects of human existence, and that this absorption nurtures their development.

For children to benefit fully from their Montessori education, it is important that parents understand the aims of the pedagogy and support the holistic development of their offspring. The same focus on nurturing the child's independence should be given at home as it is at school. It is vital that children as young as twelve to eighteen months are given time to feed, wash and dress themselves. They need access to their toys, puzzles and books, and these should be arranged on open shelves at home, as they are at nursery, so that they can be reached when the child is ready. An essential aspect of this access to activities and toys is the expectation that the child should put them back when they have finished with them. In the early stages the child's actions are not efficient. However, opportunities to practise actions and time to perform tasks bear witness to a gradual perfection of the skills, which can become second nature to a child as young as two. The newly gained competence greatly enhances each child's self-esteem and belief in their abilities, giving them the feeling of control over their lives.

Many Montessori nurseries and schools offer parent education pro-grammes. Their main aim is to make parents familiar with the Montessori approach. This does not mean teaching parents how to use the Montessori equipment – it is more a matter of introducing them to the Montessori principles as reflected in the discoveries Montessori made a hundred years ago. This means that together with the parents we need to:

- nurture the child's true potential;
- trust and respect him/her;
- provide an interesting environment which fosters freedom and independence, and from which initiative will emerge as the child matures;
- acknowledge that the freedom has to carry some responsibility in order to protect the social aspects of our lives and support the emergence of the child's self-discipline;
- give children time and consideration when planning both school and family routines and outings.

The benefit of working together with parents is that it contributes to the child's self-construction and also towards a fulfilled child and later to a fulfilled human being.

The nature and level of partnership with parents in relation to Mon-tessori settings varies from country to country. During the past twenty years much has been done in the UK to welcome parents into Montessori nurseries and schools, and to help them engage with their child's learning and development. Parents are invited to observe their children or to contribute to activities. They also participate in the children's learning by providing information about home activities and contributing to children's records and learning journeys. The recent development and use of digital technology to document children's learning and share it with their families has contributed significantly to effective communication with parents and has enhanced their understanding of their children's learning and development.

For children to benefit from this approach, parents and teachers need to work together by trusting and respecting the child's need to grow and learn in an environment favourable to individual development. There-fore it is the role of parents and teachers to prepare such an environment, one that offers activities and materials for engagement but also exudes an atmosphere of calmness, politeness and respect and brings the child close to experiences in nature.

Key points

1 The Montessori approach recognises each child as unique.
2 Montessori teachers are facilitators of children's learning. They work with parents and the wider community to ensure that learning is relevant and appropriate for each child.
3 By preparing the learning environment, they ensure that children are provided with tools for all aspects of their development.
4 The principles of the EYFS are closely aligned with those of Montessori pedagogy.
5 The Montessori approach recognises that learning needs to meet developmental needs as well as the interests of the child.
6 The activities on offer in Montessori nurseries provide children with opportunities to work towards the early learning goals.
7 The Montessori approach recognises the importance of imagination as a unique characteristic of human beings.
8 Activities and experiences at nursery develop the children's intelligence and underpin their emerging imagination.
9 Characteristics of early learning demonstrate and support the child's growing capacity to be creative and think critically.
10 Montessori settings evaluate children's learning in the context of the characteristics of early learning.

Reflections

1 Consider your approach to working with children in the context of characteristics of early learning. Reflect on children's:
   - capacity to get engaged and concentrate on an activity
   - opportunities for critical thinking
   - what you could do to promote creativity and critical thinking

2 Consider your engagement with the children in your setting:
   - how often do you work with the whole group? Critically evaluate the learning which takes place during such lessons?

- are you able to organise small group activities and how often? Are these group activities with your key children or can they be joined spontaneously? In your view what would be the benefits and challenges of such an approach?
- do you ever work with just one child? Do you ever step back and give a child an opportunity to resolve a challenge on his/her own? When and why might you choose this approach?

3 Consider sharing your experiences with your colleagues:
- do you have an opportunity for peer observations? What in your view would be the benefits of these and how would you overcome the challenges of organising peer observations?
- do you observe all the children in your setting or do you focus on your key children?
- which of the two approaches might work best for the children and why?
- do you share your learning about the children in your setting with colleagues regularly? Do you find it helpful and why? Is the sharing focused on all children or are you mostly preoccupied with the children for whom you are concerned?
- do you ever share interesting articles with your colleagues and parents? Could this sharing enhance your practice? Consider how and why.

References

BAECE (British Association of Early Childhood Education) (2012) *Development Matters*. London: BAECE.

Bowlby, J. (1969) *Attachment and Loss*. London: Hogarth Press and the Institute of Psycho-analysts.

Bruce, T. (2015) *Early Childhood Education*. 5th edition. London: Hodder Education.

DfE (Department for Education) (2017) *The Early Years Foundation Stage Framework*. London: DfE.

Goldschmied, E. and Jackson, S. (2004) *People Under Three, Young People in Day Care*. 2nd edition. Abingdon: Routledge.

Montessori, M. (1965) [1914] *Dr Montessori's Own Handbook*. New York: Schocken Books.

Montessori, M. (2007a) [1949] *The Absorbent Mind*. Amsterdam: Montessori-Pierson Publishing Company, Volume 1.

Montessori, M. (2012) *The 1946 London Lectures*. Amsterdam: Montessori-Oierson Publishing Company, Volume 17.

Siraj-Blatchford, J. and Brock, L. (2016) *Putting the Schema Back into Schema Theory and Practice: An Introduction to Schema Play.* Poole: SchemaPlay Publications. Online: www.schemaplay.com/Publications.html

Sylva, K., Melhuish, E., Sammons, P., Siraj-Blatchford, I. and Taggart, B. (2004) *The Effective Provision of Preschool Education (EPPE) Project: Findings from Pre-school to End of Key Stage 1.* Nottingham: Department for Education and Skills.

6 The favourable environment

The learning environment is the key component of the Montessori approach because it facilitates children's learning. This chapter examines some of the elements of Montessori practice introduced in Chapter 2 by providing an overview of the range of Montessori learning environments. It highlights the changes in the learning environment which reflect the age groups of children. It explains how the environment and the learning materials facilitate the child's learning. Examples of age-appropriate materials are included. The role of the teacher in context of preparation and maintenance of the environment is discussed.

> Adults admire the environment: they can remember it and things about it; but the child absorbs it. The things he sees are not just remembered; they form part of his soul. He incarnates in himself the world about him.
>
> (Montessori 2007a: 56)

The key features of the Montessori learning environment

The favourable environment prepared for the child is the key component of the Montessori approach. It is designed to promote children's development by offering them freedom of movement, choice and expression. From the Montessori (1966, 2007a, 2007b) perspective, the ability to make choices and express one's ideas supports the child's self-construction. Therefore, it is essential that the environment responds to the child's developmental needs and supports the sensitive periods. All activities are displayed, ready for use, on open shelves giving children opportunities to peruse what is available and make decision about what they want to do and with whom.

In Montessori settings children's safety is considered to be of paramount importance. Children are always shown and guided in how to use all utensils appropriately and with competence. This includes the use of scissors, knives for cutting fruit, drinking from glasses and using plates made of glass and china when children are two and three years old. Four- and five-year-olds use needles for sewing, carpentry tools and help to serve food. When they are of primary age children also help with food preparation, refine their carpentry skills and learn how to use sewing machines, potter's wheels and other craft tools. Children are afforded trust and respect while being supported by careful instruction, ongoing supervision and opportunities to perfect their skills through repetition until they become competent users of all utensils and tools in the setting.

The common characteristics of all Montessori classrooms, irrespective of the age of the children, are:

- Children are grouped vertically in family groups representing three-year age spans: toddler to three, three to six, six to nine and nine to twelve.
- Access to the outdoor classroom facilitating free flow learning in both environments.
- Adequate space to facilitate learning on the floor or at tables, which can be easily reorganised by children should they wish to do so. This is particularly salient for the birth to six age groups.
- Order supports free choice. Teachers are meticulous in ensuring that the classroom is ready for children's spontaneous use. This means that activities are organised in areas of learning and, where possible, grouped together according to the level of challenge or differentiation of learning.
- Each activity has a designated space, is accessible, complete and ready for use.
- The walls of the classroom are not overdecorated to help children focus on self-selected activities, which are organised on shelves in such a way as to engage the child's interest.
- All wall displays need to be within the child's visual field if they are intended to engage the child and if the child is expected to contribute to them.
- The activities and materials available to the children are aesthetically pleasing, well made (preferably from natural materials) and are beautiful to hold, use and look at.
- Nature should be visible in the environment, with flowers and plants

decorating the classroom. Children are given opportunities to grow and look after plants, flowers and vegetables in the garden and classroom. It is usual for children to have some pets to look after.

■ Wherever possible, children are offered real experiences as part of a three-dimensional sensory foundation for the emerging cognitive skills. Children are given access to a wide range of collections of objects such as shells or artefacts collected from different continents. These collections are often found on the nature or project table and when children express interest in them the teachers will follow up by initially engaging in conversation and later by supplementing them with books and labelled pictures to extend their interest and support learning, and to enable the writing child to document his/her learning.

■ The atmosphere of the environment is calm, relaxed and harmonious. The indoor and outdoor classrooms are hives of activity, with children engaging with the materials on their own, with friends and in small groups. The classroom is not usually silent; instead it is humming with conversation.

■ The classroom should have an area for quiet contemplation, a place where children can sit peacefully if they want to reflect or where they have a calm conversation after a squabble. In some settings they have a peace corner or peace tent, or a vase with a flower which serves as an offering to make peace with a friend. It is also possible to have a double swing in the garden where children involved in a conflict can sit and resolve their differences. The gentle motion of the swing is very soothing.

Montessori (2007a, 2007b) believed that this type of physical environment promotes engagement and fosters purposeful activity. The calmness and harmony nourish the child's spirit, which is strengthened further by adults' respect and trust in the child's ability to lead his/her learning.

Organisation of the learning environments across the ages

The infant toddler learning environment

At first glance the environment for the toddler is spacious, offering many opportunities to practise emerging gross and fine motor skills. Children may be sitting with adults on comfortable mats or carpets and sharing songs, stories and books. They may be walking up and down low steps and across a short platform. They may be painting, helping to prepare snacks, washing up and learning to choose puzzles and other activities. They have access to water activities and a sandpit. They have bicycles, carts and trolleys to push, pull and manoeuvre. There is a quiet space to rest, usually on a large mattress, where children can snuggle up should they wish to have a nap. There are opportunities for trying to do as many things as possible independently. Autonomy is the key aim at this stage of development, responding to the Montessori motto 'Help me to do it by myself'. This requires time and patience and an understanding from the adults that competence is achieved by practice and that having time to practise is an essential component of the learning environment for a two-year-old.

The activities are well spaced out on low shelves with good access for this age group. There is a designated space for each activity, and children learn to return materials to their place. However, many will enjoy doing activities standing at the shelf – this is why the spacious display of activities is important. Montessori practitioners often have more activities available and interchange them on a regular basis in order to promote further interest and develop and refine manipulative and language skills.

Activities for infants and toddlers

Whilst there are no specific materials designed by Montessori herself for this age group, Montanaro (1991) and Lillard and Lillard Jessen (2003) have suggested a range of equipment which works well for this age group and has been tested in a variety of environments. Both of these books also give ideas about a range of activities and materials to be introduced to children of this age. Activities involving pulleys, big wheels to be turned and runs into which a ball can be placed and followed, are all part of such an environment (NAMTA 1987, 1991).

Treasure baskets and heuristic play

Many Montessori infant toddler settings in the UK have introduced this age group to heuristic play, including treasure baskets and heuristic bags, as developed by Elinor Goldsmied and her colleagues in the early 1990s (Goldschmied and Jackson 2004). These materials offer opportunities for manipulation and play. The baskets support learning through sensory experiences whilst encouraging choice and giving time for exploration of textures, weights, smells and tastes from the moment a baby can sit unaided. Everyday objects such as wooden spoons, spatulas, brushes, small leather purses, key rings with a selection of keys, short lengths of chains, pieces of paper or fabric of various textures are all included in the treasure basket, as are containers with seeds or grains which serve as shakers and rattles. The opportunities to manipulate objects stimulate and reinforce specific neural pathways implicated in the development of key abilities. Current research (Robinson 2003) endorses Montessori's belief that, 'The hand is an instrument of man's intelligence' (Montessori 2007a: 185).

Montessori practitioners find that these activities engage children of this age group in a focused and sustained task for up to half an hour. Until witnessing this personally, very few adults believe such a level of concentration is possible for children of this age group. Evidence also shows that this type of activity nurtures the brain and stimulates growth of synaptic connections (Gerhardt 2004; Gopnik et al. 1999; Robinson 2003).

When babies start walking and the beginnings of language emerge, the toddlers have access to many heuristic bags. These facilitate a wide range of schematic behaviours (Athey 2007) such as transportation, enclosure, posting and trajectory whilst strengthening the child's upper body as they transport the bags around the room – an activity most young children really enjoy.

Language development

For the child's awakening sensitive period for language, babies and toddlers need to hear language spoken in everyday life. Adults need to model language by listening, responding and initiating conversations. Montessori (1966) was keen for babies and toddlers to accompany parents and carers on their shopping expeditions and also make trips to a local park or playground, in fact anywhere where the child could hear language used in an everyday context. It is also important that adults clearly name objects, using their proper name, as children engage with them – be it a bucket in the sandpit, a daisy found in the lawn, a packet of cereal found on the breakfast table or an elephant seen in a book. This expands vocabulary and as the child often repeats the name the adult has an opportunity to add a little more information or ask questions. The growing language competence enhances the child's learning and supports not only language but also cognitive development as the child grows in his/her ability to explain what they are doing, feeling, thinking or remembering.

Exposure to the singing of songs, nursery rhymes and books to look at alone or with sensitive help from adults are all essential tools for supporting the development of children's language and will be present in every Montessori infant toddler environment.

Supporting independence

Much of the children's day is occupied with meeting needs such as eating, sleeping and fresh air. During all these routines the child is given every opportunity to gain independence from adult help; therefore babies and toddlers are encouraged in feeding themselves and choosing from a range of activities around the classroom. More and more settings and Montessori practitioners work with the family to ensure that the baby's individual rhythm and daily routines are not disrupted by attending a daycare setting. They liaise with the parents and observe the children to determine the best time for them to rest and eat when ready, rather than according to specific routines within the settings. This kind of sensitivity promotes the sense of well-being from which self-esteem and self-worth emerge (Manning-Morton and Thorp 2003).

Tom's day in the infant toddler community

Tom is an eighteen-month-old boy who attends the Seedlings Montessori nursery with his older sister Anna (three years and six months old), who is in the Children's House. When they arrive in the morning they are greeted by Sneha, the manager of the setting, at the front door. Whilst Anna goes to change her shoes and hang up her coat outside her classroom, Tom's dad accompanies him to his peg and reminds him where to put his coat and gives him time to take off his shoes and put on his slippers. As they enter the infant community they are greeted by Marketa, Tom's key person, and Tom's dad gives her Tom's home book in which they share any significant events in Tom's life, both at home and at nursery. Tom kisses his dad goodbye and runs off to the mattress where John, one of the teachers, is sitting with a couple of children looking at a book. John greets Tom and invites him to join them. After a while Tom gets up and walks up the stairs, across the platform and sits on one of the steps watching Marketa greeting another family. He decides to paint a picture and remembers to put on his apron and roll up his sleeves. The paper and paints are ready for use and with a large swoop of the brush he makes a long yellow line. 'Done', declares Tom. John, who is no longer reading a story, helps him to take off the picture and puts it on the rack to dry; together they check that the easel is clean and ready for another child to use. Tom decides that the easel needs cleaning. So he pulls out a small bucket from under the easel and with a sponge wipes the easel. Some water spills and he notices and looks for the little mop which is usually propped up against the wall near the easel. He wipes the floor and decides he wants to help with the cutting up of fruit for snack.

John, who is in charge of snack preparation today, reminds Tom to wash his hands and take off his painting apron. Tom needs help with the fastening of the apron. John is ready to help and is the first one to sit next to Tom with a chopping board in front of him and a small cutlery knife ready to chop up a banana. Tom cannot help himself and tastes the banana as he cuts it. As he finishes cutting up the second banana he decides he is ready for a snack. Tom finds a small china plate, helps himself to a slice of apple, a piece of a clementine and three slices of banana, and sits next to John until all the fruit is finished. He also remembers to have a drink of water, which he manages to pour for himself into a small glass. At the end of snack he washes up at the low sinks and puts the plate and glass on the drainer. As Tom wipes his hands he decides to go outside. Marketa reminds him that he needs to change his slippers into outdoor shoes, which he can do by himself because of the Velcro fastenings and because he knows where to find them in the corridor outside the classroom. As it is a sunny spring day he does not need to put on a jacket.

In the outdoor classroom he piles up a trolley with small wooden bricks which are in the storage shed and pushes the trolley to a platform where he can build a tower. The tower topples over several times and Tom approaches Frances, one of the teachers overseeing the outdoor classroom on this day. She comes up to him and shows him how to place the bricks on top of each other very carefully. Tom has another go. Then he piles the bricks back into the trolley and pushes it towards the shed, but gets distracted by tricycles. Frances reminds him to push the trolley back near the shed. Tom finds a parked tricycle and decides to have a ride. He is approached by Jenny (four years old) who asks to have the tricycle whilst she pulls at the handle-bars. Tom shouts 'No' and Frances approaches, reminding Jenny that she will be able to have a go when Tom returns the tricycle to its parking place. Jenny runs off.

By now, it is time to go inside to join everyone for lunch. Tom likes his lunches at nursery and quickly washes his hands and sits at one of the tables next to Marketa and Ali, one of his friends who helped to set up. When the shepherd's pie arrives, he is able to help himself and starts eating. There are grapes for pudding, his favourite. Tom still needs his nap after lunch, so he waits to have his nappy changed by Marketa, then finds his cuddly and snuggles on one of the mattresses with his blanket. Gentle music is playing in the background and he soon doses off.

Marketa is there as he wakes up and reads him his favourite story about the Moon. He asks for another story, this time choosing a book of animals and joins in by making animal sounds as other children gather round for story time. At the end he goes to the shelf and chooses the farm animal puzzle. When he is done with it he returns it to the shelf and takes the basket with the animal models. He starts playing with them, putting the babies with their mummies. He helps himself to a glass of milk which is ready on the snack table, just in time to be collected by his mum. Today is his early day and he goes home before tea. Marketa has a quick chat with his mum and hands over his yellow painting and his home book to her. She waves Tom goodbye saying, 'See you tomorrow'.

The nursery, Children's House or Casa dei Bambini learning environment

The Casa dei Bambini or Children's House, as Montessori called it, should have the feeling of a house. The complete, well-set-out activities are displayed on open shelves, ready for use. Children access them and choose where to use them – on the floor, at a table, inside or outside. These arrangements of activities help children make choices. Considerable attention is given to the description of Montessori materials and activities used at this level, but Montessori's own writing does not contain a comprehensive overview of the materials.

The classroom is organised into the following areas of learning:

- Practical life or activities of everyday living
- Education of the senses
- Numeracy and arithmetic (mathematics)
- Literacy, which will include a book corner
- Cultural studies (understanding the world), which will include a nature/project table
- Creativity area (expressive arts and design)
- Outdoor learning environment

These areas of learning are elaborated in more detail below.

Practical life area/activities of everyday living

The main focus of this area is to help children develop skills which will help them to become independent. These skills are then applied to daily life in the classroom. This means that, for example, the pouring skills acquired during use of activities available on the shelf are used when serving oneself a drink, watering plants inside the classroom or in the garden, or when doing science experiments.

Most of these activities (with the exception of the dressing frames) are teacher made and developed or introduced when the teacher finds that the children demonstrate a need to learn a particular skill.

The majority of practical life activities fall under three broad categories of learning:

- Manipulative skills, which introduce activities such as:
  - pouring;
  - transferring with the use of various tongs, ladles or spoons;
  - opening and closing of boxes, bottles, locks and keys;
  - threading beads, using sewing cards and sewing with a needle, making samplers, sewing on buttons and hemming;
  - using a range of stationery tools such as glue sticks, paper clips, staplers, hole punchers and rulers;
  - folding and weaving.

- Care for the environment, which gives opportunities for learning how to accomplish:
  - sweeping, dusting and wiping inside the classroom;

- polishing of wood, glass, mirrors and metal objects;
- looking after plants inside and outside, looking after animals such as stick insects, fish and gerbils inside the classroom and rabbits and chickens outside in the garden;
- looking after the outdoor classroom by sweeping, raking leaves, etc.;
- setting a table for snack or lunch and clearing the table;
- washing dishes, washing polishing cloths and any other cloths used in the setting, use of pegs;
- gardening – digging, raking, planting and watering plants, harvesting crops;
- cooking – learning the skills of mixing, stirring, kneading dough, cutting biscuit shapes, filling cupcake cups, measuring and being aware of cooking times.

- Care of self, grace and courtesy activities which encourage children's personal hygiene and independence in dressing. Children are encouraged to:
  - take off and put on shoes, wellingtons, coats and jackets;
  - use various fastenings – Montessori developed dressing frames with buttons, buckles, hooks and eyes, zips, bows and lacings. Velcro has been added as an essential fastening gadget in the 20th century;
  - wash their hands and use the toilet;
  - brush their hair and teeth;
  - serve snack and/or lunch.

Grace and courtesy are learned best when modelled by the adults and older children. Children in Montessori settings are known for their good manners and polite behaviour. These skills are deemed essential tools for children's lives, as they demonstrate respect for themselves and others. All the activities in this area of learning reflect culturally appropriate practices.

Education of the senses

This area is the part of the classroom where most of the learning materials designed by Montessori in the first part of the 20th century can be found. They are inspired by the work of Itard and Seguin and, in the case of the geometric solids, by Froebel's Gifts (Bruce 2011, Standing 1984). Each activity focuses on a specific sensory aspect such as visual perception or identification of identical sounds, textures, shapes, colours, weights or temperature. Once the child is familiar with the objects themselves, they usually match and pair identical shapes, textures or sounds. When competent in this skill, they then focus on small differences between the objects by grading them in a specific sequence determined by the quality of the materials – such as sequencing shades of a specific colour from lightest to darkest or vice versa. Where appropriate, new vocabulary is introduced using the three-period lesson (see Chapter 3 on teaching and learning for more details).

Montessori also developed activities which enhance children's sense of taste and smell. In today's classrooms such activities are often combined with cooking activities. Montessori practitioners believe that placing these sensory experiences in the context of real activities makes them more meaningful for the children.

The sensorial activities draw on the essence of a concept they are introducing or refining (Montessori 2007a). The sensory experiences serve as a foundation for future learning and abstract thinking. The activities provide a focused model for a specific concept and as such represent an abstract idea. Montessori explains the qualities of the sensorial materials as follows: 'we can pave a way for experiences through which the subconscious mind will become imbued with these facts ... We give an abstraction ... They learn to understand the abstract concept by using the materials. We call this mechanism *materialised abstraction*' (Montessori 2012: 70).

The sensorial materials provide children with initial sensory experiences which are used later in support of more formal learning, for example the experience of sandpaper in the touch boards prepares the child for the feeling of the sandpaper letters/numerals or of the globe. Montessori refers to this as *indirect preparation*, as discussed in Chapter 3.

Education of the senses is divided into the following groups:

- Visual sense: activities in this area refine visual perception of size using tools such as knobbed and coloured cylinders, pink tower and broad stair and red rods.
- Chromatic sense activities refine visual perception of colour using: Colour box 1 (pairs of primary colours), Colour box 2 (eleven pairs of colour tablets including primary and secondary colours, as well as white and black) and Colour box 3 (seven shades of each of the nine colours found in Colour box 2).
- Tactile sense is refined with the help of touch boards and touch pairing tablets. In both activities, children are introduced to the texture of

sandpaper of various grades. These activities are further enhanced by matching and pairing of textured papers and various fabrics.

■ Auditory sense is refined with the help of sound boxes – pairs of cylinders filled with a variety of materials which, when shaken, produce diverse sounds. The child first searches for the matching pairs and later learns to use just one set and orders it along a spectrum according to the level of sound, from loud to soft or vice versa. Montessori used sets of bells (identical to those used by Mozart in *Marriage of Figaro*) which correspond in sound to all the tones and semitones found on the piano between middle C and top C. The two sets of bells are first matched by sound, or they can be sequenced following the scale of C. Older children are also encouraged to play tunes and explore combinations of sounds and also have opportunities to link the bell sounds with music notation. These activities are described in some detail in the second volume of *The Advanced Montessori Method* (Montessori 2007f).

■ Baric sense activities refine perception of weight. The Montessori baric tablets are three sets of identically shaped and sized tablets made from three types of wood, with soft wood being the lightest and hard wood being the heaviest in the set. The activity requires children to perceive small differences in weight and is based on the premise that the child already understands what heavy and light means, having had many experiences of these concepts before using the baric tablets. As this activity requires engagement of two children simultaneously, it gives them opportunities to take on the role of teacher and pupil. For this reason it is a popular activity with most children attending Montessori settings.

■ Sense of temperature is refined with the help of thermic bottles. However, these are rarely used nowadays as they require filling with hot water at specific temperatures and need to be prepared prior to the session starting in the morning. Recently, they have been replaced by thermic tablets – a set of five pairs of tablets of identical shape and size made of marble, steel, wood, felt and glass. These materials do have varying temperatures when felt but also differ in weight, so children often use them instead of the baric tablets.

■ Sense of taste and smell are closely linked and, as mentioned in the introduction to this section, are often integrated into specific cooking or food preparation activities or as part of a project focusing on our senses. If they are part of the set activities always available they require daily attention to ensure freshness.

Exploration of shapes

In addition to the specific materials for refinement of visual perception involving cubes, prisms, cylinders and rods, Montessori also developed a wide range of materials which give children opportunities for exploration of shapes. These consist of solid geometric shapes, flat shapes placed in the presentation tray and geometric cabinet and constructive triangles. These activities serve as a comprehensive introduction to the child's later study of geometry by facilitating exploration of the relationship between solid and flat shapes from which the solids are constructed. They provide children with opportunities to learn the names of shapes and investigate them in an open-ended manner.

The binomial and trinomial cubes are used as puzzles in the nursery and at primary level; they serve as introductory materials for algebra and the written formula. These activities are a good example of Montessori's ability to build on children's learning and guide them in small manageable steps towards conceptual understanding and finally, when much older, towards abstract thought. The cubes are an ideal example of what Montessori meant by materialised abstraction – they are constructed in such a way as to represent the abstract binomial and trinomial formula, yet initially the children use them as a puzzle, matching colours and shapes to make a cube.

In addition to the five senses (vision, touch, hearing, smell and taste), children in Montessori classrooms explore weight, temperature and colour. Montessori also speaks of the *stereognostic sense*, which underpins understanding of the three-dimensional shape of an object such as a cube, prism, pyramid, cylinder, ovoid, ellipsoid and sphere. Her references to the *kinaesthetic sense* refer specifically to flat shapes and their outlines, such as feeling around a circle, square and triangle. These activities are designed to prepare children for letters and numerals. They are introduced in Montessori settings with the help of sandpaper and use the multisensory approach by employing vision, touch and sound whilst exploring the outline of these figures, thus refining the kinaesthetic sense (Montessori 2007b).

Foundations for later learning

Both practical life activities and activities for education of the senses are considered to be an essential foundation for the introduction to other areas of learning in Montessori Children's Houses. The features of direct and indirect preparation underpin later learning. This does not mean that children do not return to these areas; in fact, they continue to visit them or use the skills gained from them throughout their time at nursery, and sometimes also at primary level.

A good example of direct preparation is early threading activities, highly popular with two- and three-year-olds. These activities can translate into an interest in sewing, first using sewing cards (threading laces), then being introduced to sewing with a needle, then learning to make a sampler with various stitches, and finally learning to sew on a button, make a hem or repair a hole in a garment. Thus, previously acquired skills directly prepare the child to tackle new ones.

Indirect preparation can be illustrated in the context of the child's emerging literacy skills. These skills are supported by developing eye–hand coordination, fine motor skills and flexibility of the wrist in the many manipulative activities in the areas of practical everyday living. On the 'sensorial' shelves in the nursery the children will find and get used to the feel of sandpaper. They will refine their auditory perceptions in preparation for listening to small differences in sound essential to later work with phonics, and feel around flat shapes in preparation for making letter shapes with their curved and flat lines. These various tasks, when combined, indirectly prepare the child for learning letter shapes and sounds using the sandpaper letters.

Further examples of indirect preparation are demonstrated by the child's ability to match and pair, and later sort, group and sequence the colour tablets according to shades from lightest to darkest or vice versa. These activities provide the child with skills to organise and classify information essential for later mathematical understanding and logical thinking. This is another instance of indirect preparation and demonstrates the child's capacity to think in an orderly fashion; Montessori (2007a: 169, 2012: 78) called this type of mind *the mathematical mind*.

Children use their manipulative, caring and observational skills extensively when they begin to help with gardening, explore the garden and use first-hand experiences such as sensory exploration of fruit in building their knowledge and understanding of the world. Once again, the skills of matching and pairing, sorting and grouping are used regularly in this area.

Numeracy and arithmetic

As explained above, children are introduced to mathematics and problem solving when exploring the practical life and sensorial materials. Mathematical concepts of matching, pairing, sorting and sequencing as well as estimation, symmetry and one-to-one correspondence are inherent in many of the introductory activities. They also build on the children's ability to engage in logical systematic work, which Montessori (2007a) termed the child's *mathematical mind*. It is also recognised that children in the 21st century often come to nursery with acquired knowledge of numbers and some basic recognition of small quantities such as one, two and possibly three (Allyene 2011). In most nurseries, children also use counting and numeral recognition as part of the daily routine of checking on the number of children attending, and so are familiar with the use of numbers and numerical labels for a specific purpose.

When a child demonstrates an interest in the numeracy and arithmetic materials on the shelf, they will start by learning the names of quantities and recognition of numerals before combining the two, thus making the essential one-to-one correspondence between the quantity and the symbol. Never, throughout the nursery experience, are children expected to use their counting skills without the prop of a number line, written numerals or objects to count. The sequence of activities is based on the child's learning to understand the decimal system, starting with counting to ten:

- Counting to ten. These activities include number rods, sandpaper numerals, combining number rods and numerals, spindle box and cards and counters. Only when the child understands the sequence of the numbers and their essential qualities can s/he progress. In today's Montessori classrooms there are many other activities which enhance the child's ability to count accurately to ten and possibly to twenty, such as counting puzzles and books and games. Included in the outdoor classroom can be found numbered parking places for bikes or an obstacle course which guides the child by use of numbers.
- Introduction to the decimal system using the golden bead material. This approach is unique to Montessori and is based on the idea that, when the child can count to ten, the next step should be to introduce the hierarchies of the decimal system with the help of golden beads and colour-coded numeral cards to link with the hierarchies. These activities yield an understanding of how the decimal system works and prepares the child for numerical operations of addition, subtraction, multiplication and division. In a well-run and attended Montessori classroom children around the age of four and a half to five may be introduced to these activities, provided they have the physical space to set them up and staff who believe that the children can benefit from them.

- Group operations using the golden beads. By combining the golden beads with the large and small number cards, children are given the opportunity to participate in numerical operations via a role play, where each child represents a part of the numerical sentence. For example, when taking part in addition, three children are given a set of small number cards and collect the appropriate number of beads from the bead bank. The beads and cards are arranged on a large table or floor mat. The layout of the small number cards and beads represents the equation written out and corresponds with the addition of the beads. Gradually over a period of time (spanning from nursery to primary years), children build their knowledge of number operations, and through repetition of activities memorise the answers.
- Numbers from ten to ninety-nine. These are introduced with the help of Seguin, also known as the teen and ten boards. With the help of beads and the boards, the child is given a solid understanding of the value of zero as they progress in their work from units to tens.
- Fractions. Children are also introduced to fractions with the help of fraction circles where each circle contains a different number of pieces from one to ten.

The nursery provides very solid grounding in numeracy and arithmetic, as well as opportunities to develop these skills far beyond what is usually expected of those children who display interest and aptitude in this area of learning.

Literacy

Much work is done in support of the child's emerging literacy. Montessori (2007a, 2007b) was one of the first pedagogues to highlight the importance of developing language and communication skills, and encouraged parents and carers to include their babies and toddlers in everyday life in order to develop their listening skills and to support their 'tuning into their language'. Use of rich, appropriate vocabulary and well-structured, grammatically correct sentences are encouraged by Montessori as the child progresses through his/her sensitive period for language. Exposure to books is an essential cornerstone of preparation for reading and writing. Story telling, particularly associated with the area of understanding the world, is a daily event in Montessori settings. Opportunities for emergent writing are also present in a well-organised Montessori classroom:

> The child can find an intense intellectual interest in being able to represent a word by putting together the … symbols of letters of the alphabet. It is much more fascinating at the beginning to create words from letters of the alphabet than to read them, and it is also much easier than writing them since writing involves the additional labour of mechanisms that are not yet fixed.
>
> (Montessori 2007b: 217)

Children have access to insets for design, geometric stencils which are used in a variety of ways starting with tracing of the shape and filling in the outlines. They promote pencil control and lightness of touch as well as opportunities to create patterns using their aesthetic skills. Following strong encouragement from the mothers of the children in the first Children's House (Kramer 1976), Montessori pioneered the sandpaper letters which use the multisensory approach to introduce children to letter shapes and sounds simultaneously. The knowledge of these letters is further enhanced by the use of a Large Moveable Alphabet (LMA), a set of letters of the alphabet made of wood or paper which facilitates 'writing' without necessarily requiring the skills to write. Montessori refers to these letters in the above quotation.

Using the LMA young children are able to build words based on their phonic knowledge of letters. Usually they are encouraged to start by building three-letter consonant-vowel-consonant (CVC) words such as 'dog', 'bed', 'pan', 'mud' and 'bin', gradually progressing onto initial and final blends such as 'frog' or 'belt'. In practice, with help from an adult who sounds out the individual letters of any word, children should be able to use the LMA to 'write' the names of their favourite dinosaurs, the country they visited during their summer holiday, or their names or those of their friends. These words can then be copied, if the child wishes to write them. The LMA is an ingenious tool for linking 'writing with a purpose' and preparing the child for reading, as they can 'write out messages' for their friends.

The Montessori reading scheme

The Montessori reading scheme is structured in three distinct levels and presented in a colour-coded manner:

- Pink level. As mentioned above, the children start with *three-letter words* constructed from consonant-vowel-consonant such as 'pin', 'bat', 'mug', 'pen' and 'cot'. They first build such words with the help of objects or pictures which guide them towards the possibility of working on their own as they name the object/picture and then find the appropriate letters to make up the word. They then progress onto reading, being scaffolded through onset and rhyme activities (MCI 2009), whereby children explore how many words they can make by changing the first letter to the last two such as -at (b-at, c-at, f-at, h-at, m-at, p-at, r-at, s-at). Objects and pictures are once again used to prompt identification of words. As their competence and accuracy gradually develop, children need fewer and fewer visual clues. They move from reading nouns to adjectives and verbs as they need fewer and fewer objects or images to support their initial reading skills. Phrases, sentences and books follow. Usually this level of reading in Montessori settings is identified by the materials being written on pink cards and contained in pink boxes.

■ Pale blue level. The next level, usually presented on pale blue, follows the same sequence as the pink and the child is slowly introduced to initial and final blends – such as 'pram' or 'desk'. Gradually words which include blends at the beginning and end of the word as in 'stamp' are included, words with *double letters* as in 'dress' or 'mill', and words with -ck blends, as in 'clock' or 'duck'. It is usual these days to also include the most frequently used phonemes which signify change in sound such as -sh as in 'shed' or 'dish', -ch as in 'chip', -ng as in 'king' or 'ring' and -th as in 'thin'. These phonemes act as stepping stones towards the next reading level and help the reader with sentences and reading books which accompany this level, and which are richer and more interesting than those at the pink level.

To extend reading opportunities at the pink and blue levels, *early grammar* activities can be introduced to enhance work with pink and blue level materials. The children use their reading skills whilst learning to identify parts of speech which are colour coded and so help in introducing their function and guide the reader towards appropriate sentence structures. If the children stay at the Montessori nursery beyond the age of four, and are interested in words and books, they may progress along the pink and blue level materials, and also benefit from the introduction of some of these grammar games and activities.

■ Green level. Children who stay in nursery until the age of six are likely to be introduced to the third, green, reading level – the level which causes the most difficulty because of the discrepancy between the 25 graphemes (symbols) and 44 phonemes (sounds) (MCI 2009, Morris 1990) commonly used in the English language. In the green level activities, one specific grapheme with a unique spelling is identified, such as -oo- in 'book', 'look' and 'cook', and is first explored by reading the selected words. It is then highlighted by using different coloured letters in the words built using two moveable alphabets, each in a different colour, such as green and yellow. The child progresses by using boxes with pictures, word lists, phrases and sentences and then books focusing on the one phoneme. The last activity explores different spellings of the same phoneme, as in the following examples: -ow- as in 'cow' and -ou- as is 'count'. Once again, this highlights the complexities of English and scaffolds the child's knowledge and understanding of spelling.

The reading and spelling skills of the green level are further enhanced by later grammar activities which once again mirror the early grammar activities in their sequence, adding adverbs. These materials also use a full range of vocabulary and give children opportunities to construct complex sentences, identify parts of speech and begin to understand their functions.

Understanding the world

This is an area of the classroom where teachers have the opportunity to follow the child's interests and are often challenged by the child's questions. There are many resources which can be purchased both from Montessori manufacturers and other educational suppliers for this area of learning, but originally they were teacher-made. In a well-established nursery, the resources in this area will reflect the children's expanding interests in animals, transport, space, the seasons and their families. The resources are built up as the nursery grows. The other elements which enhance this area are linked with the children's cultures, nationalities and family lives.

In a typical Montessori nursery there will be a nature table and a focus on exploration of the immediate environment of the setting, thus giving opportunities for observation and investigation of plants and animals living in the neighbourhood. In the area of geography, the child is intro-duced to the solar system, the Earth and its continents before she/he comes to explore the countries of his/her own continent. Children are given an opportunity to gain some understanding of how time is organi-sed by learning to do a daily calendar and talk about their experiences during the week and at the weekend. The child's photographic timeline and pictorial timeline of the day or of the school's week introduce children to the continuity of time and the principles of time passing.

Children also have an opportunity to explore magnets, simple electric circuits and the properties of water. These days they usually also have access to a CD player, cameras, and possibly a computer and an iPad. In addition, they may operate a microwave if the school has a kitchen at the child's level.

Nursery celebrations are closely linked with children's birthdays and various festivals relevant to the children and the teachers in the school. In nurseries where the population is homogeneous, teachers work hard to make children aware that they are part of the world and promote Montessori's ideal of each child being a *citizen of the world*. This means that children attending Montessori nurseries learn about the people of the various continents and what they eat and wear, where they live and how they care for their children. Differences are highlighted in a respectful manner, acknowledging the importance of similarities and the need for respect and acceptance of differences. Dressing-up clothes and role-play props are often linked with this area of the classroom. Artefact boxes dedicated to the seven continents contain a collection of objects such as clothes, accessories, money, CDs and books.

The Montessori practice in this area focuses on promoting human values universal to all people who live on our planet where they can be, and are very easily aligned with the British values which have become part of the EYFS regulatory framework in recent years.

It is usual for children in Montessori nurseries to learn about careful use of the planet's resources and children are introduced to recycling and repairing damaged equipment such as books.

Creativity – expressive arts and design

In a Montessori nursery children's *creative and physical development* is intrinsically linked with all the areas of the classroom described above because children can refine their movement and are given opportunities to explore and be creative. Creativity is seen broadly as a way of embracing all that the child engages in, as well as the area where children are introduced to arts and crafts, music, dancing, books and story telling. The activities are present in the nursery environment in the art area and introduce children to the skills essential for the expression of their creativity.

In the past twenty years much work has been done to promote role play in Montessori nurseries as a means of supporting aspects of children's creativity as well as their language and social skills. Over the years settings have developed this area from highly planned resources chosen and prepared by adults with all the necessary props, for let us say a shop or doctor's surgery, to a much looser organisation of this area, where basic props representing a kitchen or a bedroom are adjusted according to children's requests and following discussion of what may be needed, where it could be found and how useful it would be to their play. This approach enables children to have a much 'stronger voice' in how this area is organised whilst facilitating insights into the children's experiences and understanding of their life.

Outdoor learning environment

This is a natural extension of what happens inside the classroom and is organised and planned for children's needs and interests in line with the activities offered inside. In nurseries where free flow access between the inside and outside classroom is possible, children will follow the same routines in both environments and will be encouraged to access all areas of learning.

Once again over the past twenty years the outdoor facilities in many nurseries have been extended and developed to ensure that children use them daily, irrespective of the weather, and that activities are planned in all areas of learning, not just for physical development.

The recent growth of training for Forest School activities has contributed significantly to practitioners' understanding of the importance of children's learning outdoors. Practitioners recognise the value of a well prepared outdoor classroom which enables many children to experience learning in ways which suit their unique learning dispositions.

Anna's day in the Children's House

After Anna is greeted by Sneha on arrival to nursery she goes straight to her classroom. She knows what to do and also that her dad will come and say goodbye after he helps her little brother Tom, who is attending the infant community. She changes her shoes, hangs up her jacket and bag and enters the Children's House. Anna is greeted by Houdda, one of her teachers. She is delighted to be the first one in – this gives her the opportunity to help with fruit cutting and snack preparation. Anna enjoys helping and is quick with washing her hands before joining Frances in cutting up the fruit. She is good at chopping pears, cutting up apple wedges and carrots. She has the short sharp knife which she knows how to use when supervised by one of the adults. She also lays out the rice cakes and replenishes the raisin tin. Her dad pops in to give her a quick kiss goodbye. She is really too busy to pay much attention because she needs to make sure there are enough plates for all of the children to use and checks with Frances how many will be in class today. 'Twenty-four', replies Frances. 'That means you need to count ten places two times and then you will need four extra.' Anna follows her instructions. As she is finishing she sees her friend Tariq arrive. She runs to greet him and suggests they go and do the long rods together, just like they did yesterday, and build a maze. He asks her to wait for him whilst he says good morning to Frances, his key person. In the meantime Anna starts getting the mats ready and when Tariq joins her they begin carrying the rods over one at a time, being mindful of their length. They are very adept at creating a maze, starting with the longest rod. When ready they discuss who will start first – Anna is insistent that, as she had the idea, she should be the first one. Tariq's argument is that he is her friend and so should be able to start first. Anna is gracious and lets him start, whilst she takes her shoes off. They enjoy the balancing act and laugh as Tariq loses his balance and pushes one of the rods to the side. Other children join them, sitting round the maze, waiting for their turn. When Anna has had enough she encourages Tariq to come to the book corner to look at her favourite book – *Handa's Surprise*. As they turn pages they talk about the fruit they like. This reminds Tariq about the strawberries growing in the vegetable patch – he urges Anna to come with him to investigate if they have got any redder. They put on their outdoor shoes and off they go into the garden. The strawberries are still green – Anna comments on how long it takes for them to be ready. She sees that there is a bucket with big brushes by the blackboard and exclaims excitedly, 'Let's do painting with water!' 'I can do a big rainbow,' says Tariq. 'Look! I have done "A" for Anna and I will do "M" for mummy,' says Anna. They continue to paint using the large brushes. In the meantime Frances comes out into the garden and starts collecting some flowers for the snack table. Tariq asks if he can help her and leaves Anna. In a while Anna remembers the snack and decides to go in. After she washes her hands she serves herself a selection of everything she helped to prepare and sits next to Jasmine, who only has fruit. They begin a discussion about food and what is good for you. They are joined by Houdda, the teacher, who says she likes dates. Houdda explains that dates come from Syria, where she was born, and that they are very sweet. 'Sweets are not good for you,' says Anna. 'Sweetness is OK if it comes from fruit or honey,' comments Jasmine. Before Anna finishes with her snack she has a drink of water and then washes up the plate and glass. She checks that the place where she sat is clear and does not need a wipe.

She walks around the classroom checking out who is doing what. She decides to use the small tea set in the practical life area. As she pretends to have a tea party with her dolls she talks to herself. Then she turns to Finn, who sits next to her, and says, 'Will you come to my birthday?' He responds by asking her if she will come to his. Anna does not respond. She spills much of the water which was in the tea pot onto the table. She goes and gets a cloth and wipes up the spill before returning the tray with the tea set onto the practical life shelf. She sees Penny, one of the teachers in the art area, doing some sewing. She comes up to her and asks what she is doing. Penny explains that she is making a little sewing square, using a binka, and making crosses with her favourite thread. Anna comments that she does not like blue because purple is her favourite colour. Penny invites her to have a go. Anna declines the invitation. She needs to check if her brother Tom is in the garden. She goes up to Frances and asks about Tom, and Frances says that he has been in the garden but has gone to have a snack. Houdda comes out and sees Anna wandering around the garden. She suggests she might like to do some counting with her, since she has some lovely new pebbles that can be counted in the small numbered flower pots standing on the table next to the wall. Anna says, 'OK, how do I do it?' Houdda explains that each pot tells her how many pebbles need to be put in and when she is finished she should have none left. There are five pots (numbered from one to five) and fifteen pebbles to be counted. Anna is focused and accurate in her counting – she feels the pebbles and comments on their smoothness. Houdda says she found them on the beach at the weekend when she visited her friends who live by the sea. Anna comments that she likes the sea, but it is a bit scary sometimes – the waves can be very big in Cornwall where her grandma lives. When Anna is finished Houdda asks her if she might like to help with setting the table and getting things ready for lunch. Anna is keen, changes her shoes, washes her hands and is ready to help. Houdda finds an additional helper – Finn. Together they count twenty-four chairs and place them around the four tables, find plates and cutlery and put them on the table. They make sure the small vases with flowers are on the table and wait for Tamara to bring the food in on a trolley from the kitchen. In the meantime the rest of the children get ready for lunch. As the serving dishes with the shepherd's pie are placed on the tables, the children take their places and wait for the adults to join them and sing a song before they start eating. Each child serves him/herself a serving of the shepherd's pies. After lunch each child empties his/her leftovers into a bowl at the sink and puts his/her plate onto the kitchen trolley. Anna goes around with small plates and Finn offers the grapes to everyone from a bowl. Two other children help to clear and wipe the table. Anna, Finn and Houdda take the trolley back to the kitchen.

All the children go into the garden after lunch. Some play 'Who is afraid of Mr Wolf?' with one of the teachers, whilst other children make up their own games such as 'Mummies and Daddies'. Others ride tricycles or sit under the apple tree looking at books. At about 1.30 pm they all go inside and join Penny and a visitor who has brought a guide dog and tells them how to look after them and what they do. Finn does not want to listen to the story because he is afraid of dogs, so Houdda takes him to the book corner where they look at some books together. Three other children join them. When the visitor leaves, Anna and Tariq decide to do a big puzzle together – building the solar system. Penny talks to the children in the sensorial area where they are building a big castle using the blocks, whilst Houda is singing with a group using a 'bags of tricks' – each object in the bag reminds the children of a specific song or nursery rhyme. At 3 pm Anna's mum comes to fetch her. They say goodbye whilst Houdda comments on how helpful Anna was today. Mum and Anna go to collect Tom whilst the rest of the class get ready for their tea and play some more before their parents collect them.

Use of technology

Montessori practitioners continue to believe that young children's learning has to be rooted in first-hand experiences and that early sensory experiences and practical skills provide children with a firm foundation for later learning.

The fact that many practitioners use electronic systems to record children's learning has resulted in the presence of iPads in many settings. They have become part of daily life in the nursery, as they are part of their home life. In this way they have become tools for learning and provide opportunities to access information from the worldwide web, particularly in support of learning about the solar system and the plants and animals found on our planet. They are a source of very valuable pictorial information and provide an excellent additional learning resource. In recent years many nurseries followed the progress of Tim Peake on his journey into space – something which would not have been possible without access to the internet and an iPad to receive the messages.

At present there are not many nurseries which use specific Montessori software in place of the activities designed by Montessori. However, many nurseries do research and source activities which complement and extend the resources available in the setting. These resources are made available under the teacher's guidance and supervision. They add to the children's learning opportunities and reflect the time in which we live. The author is convinced that Montessori herself would welcome the access to information available to us today – she was keen to learn and was always at the forefront of innovation during her lifetime.

The primary school learning environment

The learning environment is once again organised in an orderly fashion into areas of learning, such as literacy, mathematics, biology, geography, history and sciences, and is accessible to the children. It is quite likely that the children will also benefit from specialist teaching and be introduced to a second language or given lessons in piano or violin playing. They may be guided through a programme of art classes introducing a range of modelling, craft or drawing techniques. There will be organised PE classes and a well-stocked library, in addition to the books available to children in their classrooms. The science laboratory and art studio are often part of a well-equipped Montessori primary school.

Most of the equipment continues to be presented on open shelves, but children also learn where to access resources such as new exercise books, replacement pens/pencils and craft and science resources. They take an active role in ensuring that the classroom is clean and orderly, often having daily or weekly responsibilities for a particular area of the classroom, both inside and outside.

The younger children (six- to nine-year-olds) have access to specific Montessori learning materials which are designed to help them acquire the basic literacy and mathematics skills essential to all further study. The one significant difference between the nursery and primary classes is the presence of exercise books, as children are expected to use them to record their learning both in their use of the English language and their growing maths skills.

The lack of formal testing under examination conditions contributes significantly to the ethos of these Montessori classrooms, where learning is spurred on by the children's natural curiosity and the facilities which promote enquiry and investigation.

For children who are fortunate enough to progress from Montessori nursery to primary school, the transition should be seamless. Many of the more advanced activities present in the nursery will appear once again on the shelves in the primary school, acknowledging the individual progress of all children and the need to revisit activities as the child's understanding of a particular topic is enhanced.

The role of the adult in preparing the environment

'The teacher's first duty is ... to watch over the environment, and this takes precedence over all the rest. Its influence is indirect but unless it be well done there will be no effective and permanent results of any kind, physical intellectual or spiritual' (Montessori 2007a: 253). The adults supporting children's learning and development in Montessori classrooms must first and foremost respect each individual child by recognising their qualities and characteristics, and trust in their developmental path as they guide the child's educational progress:

■ They must be knowledgeable and understand the unique develop-mental stages and the important role they play in contributing to the formation of the whole human being – the formation of man (Mon-tessori 2007c). This applies not only to Montessori's own view of human development, but also to the theories relating to all aspects of children's development which are available to pedagogues of the 21st century. The ability to reflect on Montessori's own understanding of children and relate this to current knowledge of child development helps Montessori teachers in their appreciation of her unique insight into children. It also gives them an opportunity to share their understanding of children with colleagues across all areas of work with children.

- They need to be comfortable in the use of specific Montessori didactic materials and understand the contribution the materials make to the child's learning.
- They must understand the principles on which the Montessori activities and materials are formulated so that they are able to extend them and develop other activities based on the same principles, such as incorporation of Forest School activities within Montessori early years settings. This knowledge also facilitates the possibility of including other commercially produced materials which enrich the children's learning and which are in harmony with Montessori's pedagogical principles, such as unit blocks in nursery classrooms.
- They must be able to observe children using diverse methods of observation and understand the specific use of these techniques in relation to the focus of the observation and its rationale.
- They must be able to analyse the observations using their developmental knowledge of children and Montessori pedagogy so that they are able to assess, plan and support the children's learning and development effectively by preparing a favourable environment.
- They must be able to reflect on their practice as well as knowledge and understanding of children. This reflection should be the basis of the teachers' ongoing professional development and personal growth, and guide them towards preparation of a more effective learning environment.

Teachers' commitment to the children is reflected in the way they prepare their classrooms:

- Their respect for the child is evident in the meticulous attention to detail when organising areas of learning, availability and completeness of activities and materials, and also in the space available for children's engagement, ensuring that there is adequate floor space, comfortable table arrangements and seating for reading or quiet contemplation. The outdoor and indoor classroom should provide a wide range of activities representing all areas of learning.

- Their trust in the children's ability to select appropriate activities for their learning, reflecting their interests and sensitive periods, is demonstrated by introducing new or extra materials and activities in support of these interests.
- Their non-judgemental approach to the activities and materials selected by individual children.
- Their understanding of the individual temperaments and rhythms of each child, which relates to the length of engagement with activities. This respect for the individuality of the child also recognises that some children have a need for active engagement in all that is taking place in the classroom, whilst other children may want to watch from a distance and learn passively by observing and mentally rehearsing what they have learned.

The above elements significantly contribute towards the harmonious ambience and generally calm atmosphere of Montessori classrooms. The teacher is the role model of the behaviours which foster such attitudes; she/he is deliberate in speech and movements and conveys kindness, consideration and consistency in expectations from the children.

Key points

1 The favourable environment is fundamental to the Montessori approach.
2 The characteristics of the environment underpin learning for all age groups of children.
3 The environment has unique qualities reflecting the ages and needs of children.
4 The environment for birth to three, three to six, six to nine and nine to twelve includes specific learning materials developed by Montessori herself.
5 The learning materials in each classroom represent curricular content.
6 The child's spontaneous choice of activities reflects his/her individual learning plan, learning dispositions and interests.
7 As children mature, they take on more and more responsibility for the daily maintenance of the classroom.

8　The role of the teacher is to prepare and maintain the environment, ready for the use of the children.

9　The teacher observes children's engagement in the classroom and plans further activities accordingly.

10　This approach requires teachers who:

- respect children and trust their ability to learn from the environment;
- understand and respect the key values underpinning the Montessori approach;
- are knowledgeable in the area of children's development;
- know how to use the Montessori learning materials;
- continue to learn themselves and as part of their practice.

Reflections

1　Consider the environment and your philosophy:

- does your setting have a philosophy which reflects the importance of the learning environment?
- what aspects of this environment are important to you as a practitioner?
- why are these aspects important to you?

2　Consider the child and the learning environment:

- how do you maximise children's individual learning opportunities in your setting?
- does the 'voice of the child' guide you when planning activities in your setting?
- what do you do when a child asks to do something which is not available/has not been planned? Apply this scenario to a child (a) with special education needs; (b) with English as an additional language; and (c) who has recently joined your setting

3　Having learned about the Montessori favourable environment:

- is there anything else you would like to introduce in your setting?
- is there an aspect of the Montessori favourable environment which you would find a challenge and why?
- if you felt strongly about introducing a new element into the environment, how would you go about sharing this with your colleagues?

4   The teacher's role in the learning environment:
   ■ how do you contribute to the learning environment in your setting?
   ■ what would you need to do if you wanted to buy or make a new piece of equipment for the nursery?
   ■ does your setting have a policy on repair and maintenance of learning resources?

5   The learning environment as part of the EYFS:
   ■ what do you understand by the term 'enabling environment'?
   ■ what do you understand by the term 'continuous provision'?
   ■ are there any links between your understanding of the above and what you have learned in this chapter?

References

Allyene, R. (2011) Even toddlers can spot when things don't add up. *Daily Telegraph*, 17 February 2011.

Athey, C. (2007) *Extending Thought in Young Children*. 2nd edition. London: Sage.

Bruce, T. (2011) *Learning Through Play for Babies, Toddlers and Young Children*. 2nd edition. London: Hodder Education.

Gerhardt, S. (2004) *Why Love Matters*. London: Routledge.

Goldschmied, E. and Jackson, S. (2004) *People Under Three: Young People in Day Care*. 2nd edition. Abingdon: Routledge.

Gopnik, A., Meltzoff, A. and Kuhl, P. (2001) *How Babies Think*. London: Phoenix.

Kramer, R. (1976) *Maria Montessori*. London: Montessori International Publishing.

Lillard, P.P. and Lillard Jessen, L. (2003) *Montessori from the Start*. New York: Schocken Books.

Manning-Morton, J. and Thorp, M. (2003) *Key Times for Play*. Maidenhead: Open University Press.

MCI (Montessori Centre International) (2009) *Literacy, Module 9*, Early Childhood Course. London: MCI.

Montanaro, S.Q. (1991) *Understanding the Human Being*. Mountain View, CA: Nienhuis Montessori USA.

Montessori, M. (1966) [1936] *The Secret of Childhood*. Notre Dame, IN: Fides Publishers Ltd.

Montessori, M. (2007a) [1949] *The Absorbent Mind*. Amsterdam: Montessori-Pierson Publishing Company, Volume 1.

Montessori, M. (2007b) [1912] *The Discovery of the Child* (originally published as *The Montessori Method*). Amsterdam: Montessori-Pierson Publishing Company, Volume 2.

Montessori, M. (2007c) [1955] *The Formation of Man*. Amsterdam: Montessori-Pierson Publishing Company, Volume 3.

Montessori, M. (2007f) [1916] *The Advanced Montessori Method – Volume 2.* Amsterdam: Montessori-Pierson Publishing Company, Volume 13.

Montessori, M. (2012) *The 1946 London Lectures.* Amsterdam: Montessori-Pierson Publishing Company, Volume 17.

Morris, J.M. (1990) *The Morris-Montessori World List.* London: London Montessori Centre.

NAMTA (North American Montessori Teachers' Association) (1987) *Montessori Under Three* (DVD).

NAMTA (1991) *Starting from Year Zero* (VHS).

Robinson, M. (2003) *From Birth to One: The Year of Opportunity.* Maidenhead: Oxford University Press.

Standing, E.M. (1984) *Maria Montessori, Her Life and Work.* New York: Plume.

7 Benefits and challenges of the Montessori approach to children's lives and communities today

This final chapter touches upon various critiques of Montessori education and reflects on the benefits of this approach to the child's individual development. It considers the challenges to delivery of Montessori education in England today. Part of the chapter makes links with current research in order to contextualise contemporary Montessori practices.

> Children come out of Montessori education understanding there is a richness and diversity to human culture and there's also a sameness. We all want love; we have families, we care about people, we do not want to live on a barren planet and we need to respect everyone's pursuit of these things. That's a basic but critical lesson of socialization, and it's something children get very well in Montessori.
>
> (Hughes in Anderson 2007)

The continued international interest in Montessori education bears witness to its relevance to children's lives and to parental support for it. The author believes that this has to do with its ethos, which is strongly focused on the individual child and recognises the child's ability to direct his/her own learning and development when nurtured in a sympathetic and carefully considered environment. In Montessori settings the accessibility and predictability of the organisation of the activities makes learning available to children and enables them to develop at their own pace, following the natural rhythm of each individual.

Montessori practitioners find that parents who have themselves experienced difficulties at school, or who have participated in a more directed outcome-based approach to education which focused on passing examinations, are looking for different ways of engaging their children in the education process. Most families still see education as a means to economic success in their child's adult life. However, they also recognise that without personal satisfaction and the ability to cope with the challenges of everyday life, their children will not flourish. Therefore, a desire for academic success, as well as social and emotional well-being of their children, supports parents' growing interest in alternative approaches to education including Montessori.

Another contributor to the growth of the Montessori approach internationally is linked to an increased understanding by governments of the importance of pre-school education as a significant factor in the laying of firm foundations for later learning and nurturing children's strong sense of self. Therefore, more attention has been given to the type and quality of services available to families with pre-school children around the world. And, whilst this sector of education remains non-compulsory, its importance cannot be understated. International interest has grown in a variety of early years frameworks and curricula such as New Zealand's Te Whariki or the Italian Reggio Emilia approach. Renewed interest in the work of the pioneers of early years education such as Froebel, Steiner, Montessori and the Forest School movement further testify to the growing recognition of the importance of children's early experiences.

In the UK research projects, such as the EPPE Project conducted by Dr Kathy Sylva and her colleagues (Sylva et al. 2004), further endorse the contribution made by early years education to children's lives, but also highlight the need for maintaining a high quality of teaching in the learning environments. All these initiatives underpin Montessori's own belief in the importance of early learning in children's lives.

In their ten-years strategy for childcare, the UK government set out aspirations for all early years practitioners to be qualified to Level 3 and each early years setting to be led by a degree-level qualified pedagogue by 2015. During the following years more than 15,000 early years professionals achieved degree-level status and funding was available for Level 3 and 4 qualifications. The need for well-prepared educators of young children was further addressed in the Tickell review. In the same year Cathy Nutbrown was asked to report on the quality of early years qualifications. After much consultation with the sector, she prepared a detailed analysis of the English workforce which coincided with a significant review of early years qualifications (Nutbrown 2012).

In 2014 universal criteria for Level 3 training of practitioners were introduced, and in September 2014 the early years educator qualifications were launched in England. This has heralded a review of Montessori training too, with MCI introducing the first nationally recognised Montessori qualification – the Montessori Diploma, birth to seven (Early Years Educator), developed jointly by MCI and the Crossfields Institute, and validated by the Northern Council for Further Education (NCFF) and the Council for Awards in Children's Care and Education (CACHE). At the time of its launch, this qualification required all applicants to the course who received funding from the government to hold a GCSE maths and English, grade C or above. The impact of this ruling has resulted in a significant downturn in registrations for all early years courses, and in spring 2017 the Department of Education lowered the entry requirements to basic skills qualification in English and maths on entry to these courses.

The early childhood degree courses, including foundation degrees, which were developed in early 2000 continue to be offered and include the Foundation Degree in Montessori Pedagogy (Early Childhood Practice) awarded by London Metropolitan University. However the focus on a degree-level-qualified early years workforce lost its momentum despite Nutbrown's (2012) recommendations. The recent review of the EYFS (DfE 2017) has kept the status quo on qualifications of leaders of early years settings, which remain at Level 3, Early Years Educator. However, greater emphasis has been placed on professional development of the whole early years workforce and personal portfolios of continuing professional development are recommended for each practitioner.

Research into the brain, its functions and impact on learning continues to dominate our current understanding of children and their development. It also confirms Montessori's early understanding of the brain and how its functions can be improved and developed in the early years though contact with the environment. Steven Hughes (2010) hails Montessori as the first pedagogue to identify the links between activity and increased brain functioning. He points out the importance of the neural pathways which are established during early years and their impact on overall cognitive development. He also highlights the benefits of the multisensory approach as facilitated by materials such as the sandpaper letters, which introduce the child to letter sounds, shapes and symbols simultaneously. Hughes considers the plasticity of the brain during the *Absorbent Mind* stage (the child's first six years of life), when *mirror neurons* are activated by imitation. Like all children at this age, those attending Montessori settings benefit from having positive role models both in the adults and their peers who lead by example. Whilst much of Hughes' research focuses on cognitive functions, he also highlights the benefits of social experiences in Montessori settings which develop children's cultural awareness and humanistic view of life.

The uniqueness of Montessori pedagogy lies in its international appeal, something that Montessori promoted throughout her life. In recent years more and more nursery schools have opened around the world. The other area of growth has been demonstrated by the development of a Montessori secondary curriculum and training of Montessori teachers in this area (see www.michaelolaf.net/montessori12-18.html). The other area where Montessori pedagogy has been applied is in support of patients with dementia – where both attitudes to the patients and their use of practical skills have brought some significant benefits (see www.alzheimers.net/2014-05-27/montessori-method-dementia/).

Interest in Montessori education continues to grow in England. Much has been done in recent years by the Montessori St. Nicholas charity to raise public awareness of Montessori education. This includes their contribution to the publication of *The Guide to the Early Years Foundation Stage in Montessori Settings* (2008, 2012), as well as continued support for the publication of *Montessori International* termly magazine.

Challenges to be addressed

Much of the current criticism of the Montessori approach is linked to limited knowledge of Montessori's own writing, as well as misuse of the Montessori approach in practice. Unfortunately, Montessori herself did not protect the use of her name in relation to Montessori teacher training or the practice undertaken by Montessori nurseries and schools. Some commentators perceive Montessori as too rigid, lacking both in opportunities for creativity and social interactions. Others see it as too relaxed and without any structure. Neither of these criticisms is accurate. Perhaps the best testimonial of what Montessori education has to offer lies with the children who have benefited from attending Montessori nurseries and schools. Their characteristics usually include sociability, creativity and imagination, ability to self-direct their actions and organise themselves and others, as well as enthusiasm for learning and commitment to their work.

Some of the misunderstandings which arise about the Montessori approach stem from Montessori's emphasis on the child's work to '*construct the adult the child will become*'. This often leads to misinterpreting the role of work and play in Montessori settings. The launch of the Early Years Foundation Stage framework (DCSF 2008) sparked further discussion about the nature of work and play in Montessori settings amongst English Montessori practitioners. Observations focusing on the nature of children's spontaneous engagement in activities offered by Montessori classrooms correlate well with the twelve features of play identified by Bruce (2015). This debate has resulted in a better understanding of the benefits of Montessori education within the early years community in general, by recently qualified Montessori practitioners and by families of children attending Montessori settings.

The lack of opportunities for role-play activities and misunderstanding of the strong Montessori emphasis on the use of real objects and real experiences as the basis for learning by young children, contribute further to the critique of Montessori practice that it is not promoting children's imagination and creativity. The lack of research evidence presented by Montessori herself and the paucity of academic research on these topics have resulted in the Montessori community not being able to answer their critics in a scientific manner. However, there is plenty of anecdotal evidence from action research by practitioners, case studies and classroom observations which demonstrates that children attending Montessori schools engage in spontaneous symbolic play, enjoy positive relationships and social interactions, and take part in activities that are full of creative imagination. In Montessori settings, well-informed adults involved in continuing professional development and who have a firm understanding of children and their needs, will be aware of these issues. These practitioners continue to base their practice on observations of children and ensure that children have every opportunity to express their unique characteristics and creative tendencies – be it through conversation and written work, problem solving, arts and crafts activities, music or dance. In these settings all aspects of children's personalities develop in an environment where they are guided by their spontaneous inner drive, interest in their surroundings and enjoyment of learning.

The 2012 publication of Montessori's *1946 London Lectures* provides evidence of the last training Montessori delivered at the age of seventy-six. The contemporary editorship of the lecture notes offers a more accessible text for all those interested in Montessori's writing and it also gives clear insights into Montessori's (2012: 172) admiration of the human capacity for creativity and imagination: 'Imagination is the true form of the intelligence of man. It is always there in this form.'

Current issues

To demonstrate the relevance of Montessori education to children's lives and the contribution it makes to society remains the biggest challenge for the Montessori movement today. It is often perceived as education favoured by the middle classes or the well-to-do in society and those who wish to buy advantage for their children. Yet this was not Montessori's vision; she wanted her method to be available to all children in the world, irrespective of their culture, race or economic circumstances.

The most powerful legacy of Montessori's pedagogy is her commitment to education for peace. She believed passionately that human beings are capable of peaceful co-existence, however, education towards such reality has to begin early – in the nursery.

The international events of the past fifteen years have reignited Montessori teachers' commitment to education for peace. The principles of such education together with practical ideas of fostering peace are well summarised in Aline Wolf's (2017) *Montessori for a Better World*. The new generation of Montessori teachers are true activists in igniting interest in young children for global citizenship, solidarity and respect for the interdependence of life on Earth. This passion is evident in Montessori teachers' support for international initiatives, such as being involved with non-governmental organisations in Africa and Asia, in their support for Syrian refugees, as well as encouraging reflection, kindness and consideration for the Earth in the daily life of their classroom.

Montessori teacher training

In practical terms, the Montessori movement remains fragmented due to the nature of teacher training. Traditionally the Montessori awarding bodies have worked in isolation, each validating their own certificates; the resulting lack of standardisation has led to poor recognition of the training by governments. Limited opportunities to take Montessori courses beyond initial training have also contributed to Montessori continuing to operate in the private sector around the world. This situation is slowly changing, with Montessori teachers in Sweden, Holland and New Zealand, for example, having to hold degree-level qualifications alongside their Montessori teacher training. Currently there are also more opportunities for Montessori teachers in the UK to attend degree-level programmes specifically designed to equip individuals to work as early years practitioners in Montessori and other early years settings.

In recent years the Montessori St. Nicholas charity has worked with several state primary schools, introducing Montessori education in their nursery and reception classes in delivery of the EYFS framework, and using some of the Montessori activities as well as principles with six- and seven-year-old children. This cooperation has demonstrated the benefits of child-led learning and the value of Montessori activities in support of developing fine motor skills used for writing, as well as offering activities to extend learning reading using the phonic approach. The Montessori numeracy activities have been much appreciated by teachers in these settings where they have been used with children who have required further support through junior school. In schools such as Aldersbrook Primary in Wanstead the introduction of the Montessori pedagogy resulted in exemplary practice.

Quality

Another element which contributes to the lack of recognition for Montessori education lies in the variations in the quality of delivery of Montessori education to children. This is particularly problematic for regulatory bodies. Various accreditation schemes have been established by Montessori organisations such as Association Montessori Internationale, American Montessori Society, Montessori Education UK and Montessori St. Nicholas charity. The last of these, through its Montessori Evaluation and Accreditation Board (MEAB), offers accreditation to schools belonging to the Montessori Schools Association (MSA). For the accreditation process to be relevant, its key focus must be to promote commitment to ongoing quality improvements in the setting and to continuing professional development to ensure that Montessori teachers keep abreast of not only local and national regulation, but also new developments in the international field of education.

The accreditation process should ensure that the key principles of Montessori education are adhered to and that positive teamwork and continued dialogue between the staff within the setting are established. Regular observations of children, the environment and teachers, both by peers and management, should be at the heart of effective Montessori practice and should encourage reflection and dialogue. This approach mirrors the evolutionary perspective advocated by Montessori herself, and is an integral part of the spiritual preparation of the teacher.

In recent years many of the Montessori settings that achieved MEAB accreditation have invested in the development of their outdoor class-rooms. These developments were often supported by funding available for such projects during the late stages of the last Labour government in the UK. These outdoor classrooms provide children with free flow access between the indoor and outdoor environments and enable some three- and four-year-olds to access learning in an optimum way. Montessori (1964: 80) herself advocated such opportunities and these developments have enriched children's learning significantly: 'my idea for the use of this open-air space, which is to be in direct communication with the school room, so that children may be free to go and come as they like, throughout the entire day'.

The other element which has enhanced Montessori nursery provision during the past ten years has been the growing interest in Forest School training. It has enabled many nurseries to offer weekly trips to woods and forests where opportunities to explore, climb trees and learn how to make fires safely encourage young children to take risks in a safe environment.

Sharing good practice

Teachers who are searching for a better understanding of children and those who are used to dialogue are better equipped to share their work with other professionals. This preparation makes a significant contribution to the accessibility of the Montessori approach to other pedagogues. Over the years the Montessori movement has been hindered by isolation and a lack of ability to share its principles with the wider education community. This may be due to ineffective communication and defensive attitudes by Montessorians who find it hard to promote and celebrate their practice when scrutinised. However, there are some excellent examples of sharing good Montessori practice in England since the government funding for early years education has made local authority professional development available to all early years providers, and since opportunities for engage-ment in early childhood degree programmes have increased.

Sadly some of these benefits have vanished as austerity measures have limited development of professional training for early years practitioners, and the access to thrity hours of 'free' nursery education in September 2017 will put significant financial and organisational pressure on nursery owners, particularly those who offer sessional provision. The Montessori community in the UK has the opportunity to engage with the MSA, which has provided not only the MEAB accreditation scheme, with the support of the Montessori St. Nicholas charity, but also continuing professional development training (both face to face and online) developed by MCI. These provisions by MSA and MCI will continue in the future.

Retaining a focus on the individual child

The focus on the individual child's developing potential is the strength of the approach and is much valued by the parents whose children attend Montessori settings. However, this focus on the individual may be one of the barriers which prevents governments from embracing Montessori education more fully. Social responsibility, supported and delivered by strong individuals, presents a real challenge not only to many teachers but also to politicians. We are still far away from the social change heralded by Montessori in her vision of a future society where individuals will act responsibly and sensitively in relation to each other and to the planet, so that society and the Earth can thrive.

Montessori education will always present a personal challenge to all practitioners and teachers. It demands respect for and trust in the child and his/her individual potential. It challenges the adult's need to teach rather than facilitate and necessitates an environment prepared with real consideration for the child.

References

Anderson, T. (2007) Neuroscience and Montessori. *Public School Montessorian*. Minneapolis: Jola Publications. Online: www.montessoripublic.org/montessoripublic/public-school-montessorian/

Bruce, T. (2015) *Early Childhood Education*, 5th editon. London: Hodder Education.

DCSF (Department for Children, Schools and Families) (2008) *Early Years Foundation Stage*. Nottingham: DCSF Publications.

DfE (2017) The Early Years Foundation Stage Framework. London: DfE. Online: www.gov.uk/government/uploads/system/uploads/attachment_data/file/596629/EYFS_STATUTORY_FRAMEWORK_2017.pdf

Hughes, S. (2010) Dr Steven Hughes discusses Montessori. Online: www.youtube.com/watch?v=LcNvTPX4Q08

Montessori, M. (1964) *The Montessori Method*. New York: Schocken Books.

Montessori, M. (2012) *The 1946 London Lectures*. Amsterdam: Montessori-Pierson Publishing Company, Volume 17.

Montessori St. Nicholas (2008) *The Guide To Early Years Foundation Stage in Montessori Settings*. London: MSN.

MSA (Montessori Schools Association) (2012) *Guide to the Early Years Foundation Stage in Montessori Settings*. London: Montessori St. Nicholas Charity.

Nutbrown, C. (2012) *Foundations for Quality: Independent Review of Early Education and Childcare Qualifications*. London: DfE. Online: www.gov.uk/government/uploads/system/uploads/attachment_data/file/175463/Nutbrown-Review.pdf

Sylva, K., Melhuish, E., Sammons, P., Siraj-Blatchford, I. and Taggart, B. (2004) The Effective Provision of Preschools Education (EPPE) Project, in J.J. van Kuyk (ed.) *The Quality of Early Childhood Education*. Arnhem, The Netherlands: Cito (pp. 46–54).

Wolf, A.D. (2017) *Montessori for a Better World*. USA: Parent Child Press, division of Montessori Services.com.

Appendix **Montessori secondary education – the *Erdkinder* (land-children)**

1

Very few children have the opportunity to benefit from Montessori secondary education.

In the majority of Montessori schools for twelve- to sixteen-/eighteen-year-olds, learning follows the requirements of the curriculum of the state or country in which they are living. They may also benefit from access to a farm (for example Hershey Montessori Farm School) or from a range of workshops, helping them to develop skills which will lead to employment such as in car repair or pottery workshops. However, the ethos of a deep understanding of the nature of the young person and trust in their ability to make the right decisions not only for themselves, but also in relation to the community in which they are living, remains embedded in the principles and aims of the school. This approach continues to nurture a strong individual with a sense of personal worth and social responsibility.

Erdkinder classrooms and organisation of learning

Montessori's (2007e) recommendations for education of secondary-school-age children recognise the child's tremendous physical changes and need to establish their identity alongside their peers. She recommends a special kind of boarding school where boys and girls would be engaged in learning about academic subjects through practical tasks. For example, chemistry could be learned whilst fertilising fields or preparing glazes for pottery.

She believed that children of this age are better served by practical work rather than academic study, and applying theoretical knowledge to practical tasks to be their best preparation for life. For instance, they would learn about economics by managing the finances of a hotel for visiting parents or selling the agricultural produce and craft artefacts the school would grow or manufacture.

Whilst many adults agree that this would have been an ideal preparation for their own lives and that learning a trade and being apprenticed to a craftsman would have been exactly what they needed, persuading parents to invest in this type of education for their children is a real challenge. Currently there are no secondary schools which embrace Montessori's recommendations fully, without a concern for the academic curriculum.

In recent years, Montessori's views on education of this age group have been revised. David Khan and Betsy Coe, in the US, made a particular contribution to this review. They have developed a secondary Montessori curriculum which combines Montessori ideals of teenagers engaging in and running a farm with the secondary curriculum requirements of the state in which their schools operate. Their approach has been adopted by schools in Sweden, Germany and South Africa. Conversely, in countries like Holland, the children in Montessori secondary schools follow the national curriculum with the ethos of Montessori's work – that of respect and consideration for each other and the planet – rather than her practical recommendations.

Erdkinder learning environment

Young people of this age group need access to specialist classrooms such as a science lab, art studio or drama workshop, whilst teenagers benefit from opportunities to help on a farm, in an artist's studio or with the running of a business, in addition to having a classroom space conducive to their learning.

Montessori secondary education recommends that both genders share a home located in the countryside. Montessori saw this experience as a significant contribution towards young people's preparation for adult life whilst acquiring knowledge and understanding of themselves and their environment. Ideally she envisaged these young men and women living together in a hostel. They would be 'looked after' by a married couple – the house 'father' and 'mother'. This hostel would be located on a large estate, possibly in the middle of the woods or near the sea. Some of the teachers would be living in the school and, together with the house parents, would be responsible for the set code of conduct until self-discipline became established within the community. The appropriately qualified teachers would be supported by technical instructors who would guide the young people in developing the practical skills essential for adult life.

Today's Montessori secondary schools ensure that the young people attending are given the academic grounding which will enable them to progress with university studies if they so desire. However, the emphasis remains on the principle of the curriculum being 'drawn up gradually under the guidance of experience' (Montessori 2007a: 71).

Learning in *Erdkinder* schools

Young people attending Montessori secondary schools develop social skills and new levels of personal independence and responsibility, which are an essential part of this stage of their life. There are no specific Montessori learning materials for this age group – the curriculum has evolved in line with the national requirements of the specific countries participating. However, the common thread is continued respect for the young person and for the environment, not only that of the school but also the community, the country and the planet.

Montessori (2007e) identified two key components when considering the education of young people in the *Erdkinder* schools: the moral and physical care of the pupils, and the syllabus and methods of study. Both are determined by the developmental level of the individual. Montessori related moral care to the utmost respect for the young person, adults and environment, and physical care to the maintenance of their well-being – both psychological and physical. These two aspects of the individual's development guide the structure of the syllabus and the methods of study, identified as three distinct strands (Montessori, 2007e):

1 Opportunities for self-expression, which guide the complex development of personality in expressing one's imagination and creativity through music, drama and art.
2 Education in relation to intellectual (psychic) development. In this context Montessori considers three key subjects: moral education (which in today's context relates to personal and social development as identified by the citizenship studies included in the UK secondary curriculum), mathematics and languages.
3 Preparation for adult life, which is further organised (Montessori 2007e) into:

- study of the Earth and living things in relation to biology, geography, cosmology and astronomy;
- study of human progress in relation to scientific discoveries in physics, chemistry, engineering and genetics;
- study of the history of mankind.

In this area, the study must relate to facts of everyday life and should be 'tested and confirmed by observation or experiment' (Montessori 2007e: 76–77). Montessori (2007e) believed that all children, irrespective of their prior education, would benefit from this approach to secondary education, and that children with identified psychological problems would thrive in this type of school. To find out more about today's *Erdkinder* initiatives see North American Montessori Teachers Association (NAMTA) resources.

Montessori's view of university education

For Montessori (2007e), university education needed to have a higher purpose, helping human beings in their moral, intellectual and social growth and taking into consideration previous education received and the characteristics of the individual. She reflected on the purpose of universities in medieval times when they were 'central instruments of progress and civilisation' (Montessori 2007e: 84). She felt that, increasingly, modern higher education was losing its sense of vision and purpose. She saw universities of the 20th century as places which extended young people's period of study and prolonged economic dependence on families, rather than being a creative force within society.

According to Montessori (2007e: 84), university education should be a natural progression of the development of a human being:

If the 'formation of man' becomes the basis of education, then the coordination of all schools from infancy to maturity, from nursery to university, arises as a first necessity: for man is a unity, an individuality that passes through interdependent phases of development. Each preceding phase prepares the one that follows, from its base, nurtures the energies that urge towards the succeeding period of life.

2 Appendix Glossary of terms

Absorbent mind – The unique quality of the human mind, most acute from birth to six, when the child learns by absorption and synthesis of stimuli from the environment.

Adaptation – Characteristic ability of all human beings to adapt to new experiences, conditions and circumstances of life. It is inherent in Montessori's notion of cosmic education, and is an integral part of her evolutionary perspective.

Auto-didactic – Term used by Montessori to describe the qualities of the Montessori learning materials which enable children to teach themselves.

Cohesion of the social unit – Describes the stage of the child's development when she/he has a sense of belonging to a community, and ability to consider the needs of the group and place them before her/his own needs and wants. For further explanation see the characteristics of the conscious absorbent mind.

Conscious absorbent mind – The second stage of the absorbent mind, usually associated with the beginning of nursery education because the child is able to express basic needs through language and is capable of independence in dressing and personal hygiene. The child's ability to control his/her inner urges gradually wanes and the child begins to demonstrate the ability to use his/her will and demonstrate emerging awareness of socially appropriate behaviour.

One of the two sensitive periods, the characteristic of the conscious absorbent mind highlights the social aspects of life when the child is able to absorb and mirror social mores of his/her culture, and when awareness of the needs of others gradually emerges as the child de-centres. This sensitive period is closely linked with the child's *normalisation*, which is often referred to as the 'socialisation process'. During this stage of his/her life the child becomes conscious of the nursery community – Montessori refers to this as the *cohesion of the social unit.*

The sensitive period for refinement of the senses is also evident at this stage of the child's life and is supported by the use of sensorial materials which scaffold the development of the child's conceptual understanding of the world and the emerging ability to organise and classify information, explore and problem solve. All these aspects of the sensitive period, combined with the child's growing language skills, significantly contribute towards the child's cognitive development and demonstrate the emerging creative thinking.

Cosmic education – A key element of Montessori primary education, cosmic education underpins the delivery of the curriculum. Its key element is the theory of evolution as explained in the Great Lessons. The Lessons highlight the ongoing change within the cosmos and the interdependence of all existence on our planet. Adaptability of all species is also considered, as is our responsibility for the future of the Earth.

Control of error – A device developed by Montessori which gives the child an opportunity to perceive his/her error as manifested in all activities which are designed on the principle of one-to-one correspondence. Older children have control cards which give them the opportunity to check the correctness of their answers in solving mathematical and grammar challenges.

Creativity – Relates to all opportunities given to children to explore, problem solve, think for themselves and express their thoughts, feelings and ideas. It is inherent in all that the child does. It is perceived as the natural outcome of the child's learning in a Montessori setting because the child is given the opportunity to learn from the environment, along with sensitive support from an adult.

Cycle of activity – Describes any activity the child undertakes in a Montessori setting. It begins with a decision to do something, finding the activity either inside or outside the classroom (usually found on an open shelf for easy access) and engaging with it for as long or as little as the child needs to. The cycle is finished when the activity is returned to the shelf, ready for another child to use.

Deviations – In the Montessori context deviations are behaviours which develop as a result of the child's inability to follow the natural, spontaneous path of development. They are identified in the context of the child's normalisation (see below). According to Montessori most children experience some of these conditions, which hinder natural development.

Great Lessons – These are the backbone of the Montessori classic primary curriculum. They are the tools for the delivery of Montessori's vision of cosmic education. They explore the history of life on Earth, emergence of human beings, early civilisations and the history of written language and mathematics.

Horme – The inner drive which guides the very young child in his/her learning and development. Montessori also refers to the *hormic impulse*, which drives the child toward actions and independence.

Human tendencies – These are the unique and genetic characteristics of all human species. Montessori includes orientations (in relation to spatial and environmental awareness and sense of order) gregariousness, adaptation, communication and imagination. These tendencies are manifested in children's sensitive periods.

Imagination – Imagination is a unique tendency characterising the human species. Montessori believed that imagination is best cultivated through real experiences as evident in children's spontaneous role play, when scenarios from daily life are re-enacted. She believed that contact with nature and sensory experiences are the best guide in supporting children's emerging imagination.

Mathematical mind – A characteristic of the human mind which is capable of organised logical thinking and classification of information. The sensorial materials available to children in Montessori settings cultivate these aptitudes and prepare the child for later study of mathematics.

Materialised abstractions – A term that Montessori related to the qualities of the sensorial materials which enable the child to establish conceptual understanding of the environment.

Mneme – A genetic memory present in all living beings: plants, animals and humans. It is closely linked with our ability to adapt to new conditions of life and is evident in our instincts. Montessori believed that in the spiritual embryonic stage the instincts that were present at birth become manifested as our potentialities. How these potentialities develop will very much depend on the conditions present in the child's immediate environment.

Nebulae – Montessori borrowed this term, as she did with the *horme*, from cosmology. For Montessori, the nebulae are synonymous with human potentialities. They lie dormant, waiting for the right moment to emerge. They are closely linked with the sensitive periods.

Normalisation – This term does not imply that the child is abnormal. In the Montessori context it means that the child is provided with conditions which enable him/her to follow a natural/normal path of development. Normalisation is a process of socialisation during which the child gets accustomed to life at the nursery. If the conditions are right, the child begins to demonstrate the characteristics typical of every child who is given time to engage with the environment and develop naturally and spontaneously according to his/her individual rhythm and inner guide.

Planes of development – Stages of growth accompanied by their typical characteristics. Each stage is unique and essential for maturation, contributing to development in the next stage. There are three key stages: birth to six (the stage of the absorbent mind), six to twelve (the childhood stage) and twelve to eighteen (the adolescence stage). Each stage is subdivided into three-year spans.

Play – Play is often called 'work' in Montessori settings because it contributes to the child's development. It is any activity spontaneously chosen by the child or a group of children which absorbs their whole being.

Sensitive periods – These are times of special sensitivity to the development of skills essential for life. These periods fully absorb the child. They are not linear and usually overlap. Those which are most evident in the first three years of life are sensitivity to movement, language, acquisition of skills for organisation (order) and noticing small detail, whilst skills for refinement of the senses or developing social aspects of life are prominent from about three years onwards. When these special traits appear, it is essential that they are nurtured and supported so that they reach their optimum level. When the sensitivity passes, the acquisition of these skills will no longer come as naturally to the child.

Adults should look out for the signs of sensitive periods and provide an environment which will facilitate their attainment.

Social embryo – Montessori uses the analogy of a physical embryo because she sees both the social and spiritual embryonic stages as periods of transformation. The social embryonic stage is synonymous with the stage of the conscious absorbent mind (between three and six years of age). At this stage the child emerges as a social being with a keen interest in the social conventions of his/her culture. The child also begins to be less egocentric and displays an ability to consider the needs of others and put them in front of his/her own. At the end of this period of socialisation (around the age of six), the child should be socially aware and enjoy being part of a group. In most countries this is the age when a child enters compulsory education in a primary school.

Spiritual embryo – Sometimes referred to as a psychic embryo, this is the time when the child's unique spirit/personality emerges. It corresponds with the unconscious absorbent mind, during which the *horme* drives the child's actions towards independence and sensitive periods emerge.

Unconscious absorbent mind – This corresponds with the child's first three years of life, when the child is driven by the hormic impulse, when his/her personality unfolds and the sensitive periods become pronounced. It is essential that the child is treated with the utmost patience, sensitivity and care during this first formative period in his/her life.

Volition/will – Relates to the child's will, which becomes evident toward the end of the spiritual embryonic stage. It is vital that children are given opportunities to manage their learning in an atmosphere of freedom which also contains some element of responsibility. Adults must be careful not to dominate young children's decision making and not substitute the child's needs and desires with their own. Too much adult control is damaging to the spirit of the child and prevents the development of self-discipline, which is the key to the socialisation of the child during the first six years of life.

Work – Perceived by Montessori as the totality of the child's efforts which contribute to the formation of a mature human being.

Work-cycle – This is a period of time (usually two and half to three hours, extending to four hours in primary classrooms) during which the child has the opportunity to spontaneously engage with a wide variety of activities on offer in the classroom. These activities may be solitary, with a friend, in a small group of friends or with an adult. The key is that the activities are decided upon by the child. Provided the well-being of the group is respected, the child is free to decide on what to do and with whom. This is possible because all the activities included in the favourable environment are beneficial to the child. The work-cycle is one of the key elements which contribute towards the child's developing self-discipline and socialisation.

3 Appendix Key Montessori texts

Readers of all Montessori books need to be aware that, with the exception of *The Montessori Method*, most of the Montessori texts are a collection of lectures, later edited for publication. Not all of the text in English was translated from Italian; some of the books have their origins in French. Over the years, several editions of the same book may have been published – some authorised by the Montessori family and some not. The books reflect the time of first publication; in an endeavour to retain the original ethos they have not been edited or brought up to date in terms of language usage. As a result, they are sometimes difficult to understand, repetitious and prone to language which seems unacceptable to today's readers. A lack of proper indexing contributes to further difficulties with the accessibility of the text. Nonetheless, the texts give us a very clear insight into Montessori's attitudes to children and to her philosophy, out of which sprung her pedagogical views.

Books written by Maria Montessori

Montessori, M. (1964) [1912] *The Montessori Method.* New York: Schocken Books.
The first book written by Montessori, providing an insight into her original ideas.

Montessori, M. (1965) [1914] *Dr Montessori's Own Handbook.* New York: Schocken Books.
This handbook gives us an overview of the early use of Montessori's learning materials and identifies some of the changes which occurred later.

Montessori, M. (1966) [1936] *The Secret of Childhood*. Notre Dame, IN: Fides Publishers Ltd.
This book provides a relatively accessible reading of the principles which underpin Montessori's writing about young children.

Montessori, M. (2007a) [1949] *The Absorbent Mind*. Amsterdam: Montessori-Pierson Publishing Company, Volume 1.
This book is considered by many as the key text to understanding Montessori's philosophy and covers similar topics addressed in *The Secret of Childhood*, particularly relevant to the youngest children from birth to three years of age.

Montessori, M. (2007b) [1912] *The Discovery of the Child* (originally published as *The Montessori Method*). Amsterdam: Montessori-Pierson Publishing Company, Volume 2.
As indicated above, this text is a revision of *The Montessori Method* and gives the reader the opportunity to trace changes in Montessori's views and attitudes between 1912 and the late 1940s when it was published for the first time. It focuses more on pedagogy and gives a description of several aspects of the Montessori early childhood curriculum. Considered to be one of the key texts used in Montessori teacher training alongside *The Absorbent Mind*.

Montessori, M. (2007c) [1955] *The Formation of Man*. Amsterdam: Montessori-Pierson Publishing Company, Volume 3.
This text explains the basics of the Montessori approach and also addresses issues of world literacy in the chapter of the same name.

Montessori, M. (1989a) [1961] *What You Should Know About Your Child*. Oxford: ABC – Clio Ltd, Volume 4.
A guide for parents and teachers exploring Montessori's view of the physical and mental development of the child. It is based on lectures given in Sri Lanka in 1948.

Montessori, M. (1989b) [1946] *Education for New World*. Oxford: ABC – Clio Ltd, Volume 5.
Written at the end of World War II, this is a summary of Montessori's view of the young child and explores the role of education in the changing world.

Montessori, M. (1989c) [1979] *The Child, Society and the World.* Oxford: ABC – Clio Ltd, Volume 7.
A collection of lectures and speeches made by Montessori on education and the child in society.

Montessori, M. (1989d) [1975] *The Child in the Family.* Oxford: ABC – Clio Ltd, Volume 8.
This text relates to the needs of the child in the second stage of development (six to twelve years old) and explores the underlying principles of Montessori's cosmic education.

Montessori, M. (1991) [1918] *The Advanced Montessori Method – Volume 1.* Oxford: ABC – Clio Ltd, Volume 9.
Montessori explains and expands on the education of children from three to six years of age. Some of the ideas introduced in *The Absorbent Mind* and *The Discovery of the Child* are particularly relevant.

Montessori, M. (1992) [1949] *Education and Peace.* Oxford: ABC – Clio Ltd, Volume 10.
This is a collection of speeches and lectures presented by Montessori during the 1930s, when she promoted her ideals of children being the agents of change. The documents bear testament to Montessori's later nominations for the Nobel Peace Prize in 1948.

Montessori, M. (2007e) [1948] *From Childhood and Adolescence.* Amsterdam: Montessori-Pierson Publishing Company, Volume 12.
This volume describes Montessori's developmental view of children at the primary school age (six to twelve year olds) and also includes her essay on *Erdkinder* (education for secondary-school-age children, twelve to eighteen years old).

Montessori, M. (2007f) [1916] *The Advanced Montessori Method – Volume 2.* Amsterdam: Montessori-Pierson Publishing Company, Volume 13.
This volume describes the curriculum appropriate for primary-school-age children, focusing both on materials and techniques relevant to this age group.

Montessori, M. (1997a) [1976] *Basic Ideas of Montessori's Educational Theory.* Oxford: ABC – Clio Ltd, Volume 14.
This is a collection of extracts from Montessori's writing and teaching translated from German and compiled by Paul Oswald and Gunter Schulz-Benesch.

Montessori, M. (2007b) [1912] *The Discovery of the Child* (originally published as *The Montessori Method*). Amsterdam: Montessori-Pierson Publishing Company, Volume 2.
As the title indicates, this is a collection of lectures given by Montessori during her visit to the US in 1915.

Montessori, M. (2012) *The 1946 London Lectures.* Amsterdam: Montessori-Pierson Publishing Company, Volume 17.
This volume includes the last training course delivered by Montessori in London in 1946. This volume is edited by Dr Annette Haines and offers a significant insight into Montessori's ideas about education of young children at the end of her career.

Montessori, M. (2013) *The 1913 Rome Lectures First International Training Course.* Amsterdam: Montessori-Pierson Publishing Company, Volume 18.
This volume documents the first training course delivered by Montessori in Rome in 1913 and offers the reader an opportunity to compare her ideas with the 1946 London course. It is edited by Dr Susan Freez and demonstrates that from the very beginning Montessori saw the child as an agent of change.

Contemporary publications about Maria Montessori and her pedagogy

Duffy, M. and Duffy, D. (2002) *Children of the Universe: Cosmic Education in the Montessori Elementary Classroom.* Hollidaysburgh, PA: Parent Child Press.
As the title suggests, this book explains the principles of cosmic education and offers practical ideas for delivery of primary curriculum underpinned by these principles.

Freez, S. (2010) *Montessori and Early Childhood.* London: Sage.
This book examines the influence of pioneering work by Maria Montessori by providing an overview of her pedagogy and practice in the context of today's research in the fields of neuroscience and child development.

Giardiello, P. (2013) *Pioneers of Early Childhood Education: The Roots and Legacies of Rachael and Margaret McMillan, Maria Montessori and Susan Isaacs.* **Abingdon: Routledge.**
This book examines the contributions to British early childhood education made by four women who worked with young children between the two world wars in the 20th century.

Isaacs, B. (2015) *Bringing the Montessori Approach to Your Early Years Practice.* **3rd edition. Abingdon: Routledge. David Fulton Book.**
This is a comprehensive guide to the principles of Montessori education and their impact on our practice today. It examines the EYFS and its implications for Montessori practice in England and international settings which follow both the English curriculum and Montessori approach.

Kramer, R. (1976) *Maria Montessori.* **London: Montessori International Publishing Ltd.**
This is a well-researched and critical biography of Maria Montessori, placing this pioneer of early childhood education in the context of 20th-century history and the emerging celebration of the child as the herald of our future.

Lillard and family (also see the text by Stoll-Lillard)
In four volumes, Paula Polk Lillard, one of the most consistent contemporary writers on Montessori education, charts her work with children and her understanding of Montessori philosophy and pedagogy from birth to the age of twelve.

Lillard, P.P. (1972) *Montessori, a Modern Approach.* **New York: Schocken Books.**
Focusing on work with nursery-age children.

Lillard, P.P. (1980) *Montessori in the Classroom.* **New York: Schocken Books.**
Describes Lillard's early days as a Montessori teacher.

Lillard, P.P. (1996) *Montessori Today.* **New York: Schocken Books.**
Focuses on primary-school-age children.

Lillard, P.P. and Lillard Jessen, L. (2003) *Montessori from the Start.* **New York: Schocken Books.**
Written with her daughter-in-law, Lillard addresses care and learning of the youngest children.

Loeffler, M.H. (ed.) (1992) *Montessori in Contemporary American Culture.* **Portsmouth, NH: Heinemann.**
The many essays included in this book offer an informed glimpse at the many aspects of Montessori education in the US at the end of 20th century by Montessorians and their mainstream colleagues. Contributions made by Lillian Katz, David Eldkin and Carol Chomsky provide opportunities for further engaged discussion as Montessori education thrives in the 21st century in the US and internationally.

Montessori, M. Jnr (1992) [1976] *Education for Human Development.* **Amsterdam: Montessori-Pierson Publishing Company, Volume 11.**
This book is written by Montessori's grandson and provides an insight into her personality, philosophy and pedagogy.

Montanaro, S.Q. (1991) *Understanding the Human Being.* **Mountain View, CA: Nienhuis Montessori USA.**
Montanaro's contribution to Montessori's own views on the nurture of the newborn provides a contemporary practical guide for parents and practitioners.

O'Donnell, M. (2014) *Maria Montessori: Critical Introduction to Key Themes and Debates.* **London: Bloomsbury.**
This book explores key aspects of Montessori education and considers the implications for Montessori education in the context of education today, including views of its critics and supporters.

Standing, E.M. (1984) *Maria Montessori: Her Life and Work.* **New York: Plume.**
This is the official biography of Maria Montessori, endorsed by her, which aims to explain the key principles of her philosophy and pedagogy.

Stoll-Lillard, A. (2008) *Montessori: The Science of Genius.* **New York: Oxford University Press.**
This book examines the contribution made by Montessori to today's understanding of children, and it is supported by the author's research.

Wolf, A.D. (2017) *Montessori for a Better World.* **USA: Parent Child Press, division of Montessori Services.com.**
This is a collection of writings and presentations by Aline Wolf which reflects on how to nurture the spirit of the child and develop harmonious and respectful attitudes towards life on our planet.

Appendix **Leading UK and international Montessori organisations**

UK Montessori organisations

Montessori Education UK Ltd
21 Vineayrd Hill, Wimbledon, London SW19 7JL
www.montessorioeducationuk.org

Montessori Evaluation and Accreditation Board
38 Marlborough Place, London NW8 0PJ
www.montessori.org.uk/msa schools/accreditation

Montessori Schools Association
38 Marlborough Place, London NW8 0PJ
www.montessori.org.uk/msa schools

Montessori Society (AMI) UK
26 Lyndhurst Gardens, London NW3 5NW
www.montessori-uk.org

Montessori St. Nicholas charity
38 Marlborough Place, London NW8 0PJ
www.montessori.org.uk

UK Montessori teacher training

Bournemouth Montessori Centre
81 Landsdowne Road, Bournemouth BH1 1RP
www.bournemouthmontessori.co.uk

Maria Montessori Institute
126–134 Baker St, Marylebone, London W1U 6SH
www.mariamontessori.org

Montessori Centre International
38 Marlborough Place, London NW8 0PJ
www.montessori.org.uk

Montessori Partnership
www.montessoripartnership.com

International Montessori organisations

American Montessori Association
281 Park Avenue South, NY, NY 10010, USA
www. amshq.org

Association Montessori Internationale
Koninginneweg 1611075, CN Amsterdam, The Netherlands
www.ami-global.org

North American Montessori Teacher's Association
www.montessori-namta.org

The Montessori Foundation
www.montessori.org

Bibliography

Allyene, R. (2011) Even toddlers can spot when things don't add up. *Daily Telegraph*, 17 February.

Anderson, T. (2007) Neuroscience and Montessori. *Public School Montessorian*. Minneapolis: Jola Publications. Online: www.montessoripublic. org/montessoripublic/public-school-montessorian/

Athey, C. (2007) *Extending Thought in Young Children*. 2nd edition. London: Sage.

BAECE (British Association of Early Childhood Education) (2012) *Development Matters*. London: BAECE.

Bowlby J. (1969) *Attachment and Loss*. London: Hogarth Press and the Institute of Psychoanalysts.

Britton, L. (1998) *Montessori: Play and Learn*. New York: Vermillion Press.

Bruce, T. (1991) *Time to Play in Early Childhood Education*. London: Hodder and Stoughton.

Bruce, T. (2011) *Learning Through Play for Babies, Toddlers and Young Children*. 2nd edition. London: Hodder Education.

Bruce, T. (2015) *Early Childhood Education*. 5th edition. London: Hodder Education.

Bruner, J. (1960) *The Process of Education*. Cambridge, MA: Harvard University Press.

Chattin-McNichols, J. (1992) *The Montessori Controversy*. New York: Delmar Publishers Inc.

Covington Packard, R. (1972) *The Hidden Hinge*. Notre Dame, IN: Fides Publishing, Inc.

DCSF (Department for Children, Schools and Families) (2008) *Early Years Foundation Stage*. Nottingham: DCSF Publications.

Dewey, J. (1944) *Democracy and Education*. New York: Free Press.

DfE (Department for Education) (2012*) Statutory Framework for Early Years Foundation Stage*. London: DfE.

DfE (2017) *The Early Years Foundation Stage Framework*. London: DfE. Online: www.gov.uk/government/uploads/system/uploads/attach ment_data/file/596629/EYFS_STATUTORY_FRAMEWORK_2017.pdf

Doherty, J. and Hughes, M. (2009) *Child Development: Theory and Practice 0–11*. Harlow: Pearson Education Ltd.

Duffy, M. and Duffy, D. (2002) *Children of the Universe: Cosmic Education in the Montessori Elementary Classroom*. Hollidaysburgh, PA: Parent Child Press.

Erikson, E.H. (1940) *Childhood and Society*. New York: W.W. Norton.

Freez, S. (2010) *Montessori and Early Childhood*. London: Sage.

Gerhardt, S. (2004) *Why Love Matters*. London: Routledge.

Gettman, D. (1987) *Basic Montessori: Learning Activities for Under-Fives*. Oxford: ABC Clio Ltd.*

Giardiello, P. (2013) *Pioneers of Early Childhood Education: The Roots and Legacies of Rachael and Margaret McMillan, Maria Montessori and Susan Isaacs*. Abingdon: Routledge.

Goldschmied, E. and Jackson, S. (2004) *People Under Three, Young People in Day Care*. 2nd edition. Abingdon: Routledge.

Gopnik, A., Meltzoff, A. and Kuhl, P. (2001) *How Babies Think*. London: Phoenix.

Hainstock, E. (1978) *Essential Montessori*. New York: Plume Books.

Holt, J. (1967) *How Children Learn*. London: Penguin.

Hughes, S. (2010) Dr Steven Hughes discusses Montessori. Online: www.youtube.com/watch?v=LcNvTPX4Q08

Isaacs, B. (2015) *Bringing the Montessori Approach to Your Early Years Practice*. 3rd edition. Abingdon: Routledge. David Fulton Book.

Isaacs, S. (1968) *The Nursery Years*. London: Routledge & Kegan Paul.

Itard, J.M. Gaspard (1801) *The Wild Boy of Aveyron*. Online: https://owl cation.com/social-sciences/The-Wild-Boy-of-Aveyron

Jenkinson, S. (2002) *The Genius of Play*. Stroud: Hawthorn Press.

Kramer, R. (1976) *Maria Montessori*. London: Montessori International Publishing.

Laevers, F. (ed.) (1994) *Defining and Assessing Quality in Early Childhood Education*. Belgium: Leuven University Press.

Lawrence, L. (1998) *Montessori: Read and Write*. London: Ebury Press.

Liebeck, P. (1984) *How Children Learn Mathematics*. London: Penguin.

Lillard, P.P. (1972) *Montessori, a Modern Approach*. New York: Schocken Books.

Lillard, P.P. (1980) *Montessori in the Classroom*. New York: Schocken Books.

Lillard, P.P. (1996) *Montessori Today*. New York: Schocken Books.

Lillard, P.P. and Lillard Jessen, L. (2003) *Montessori from the Start*. New York: Schocken Books.

Loeffler, M.H. (ed.) (1992) *Montessori in Contemporary American Culture*. Portsmouth, NH: Heinemann.

Macleod-Brudenell, I. and Kay, J. (2008) *Advanced Early Years Care and Education*. 2nd edition. Oxford: Heinemann.

Manning-Morton, J. and Thorp, M. (2003) *Key Times for Play*. Maidenhead: Open University Press.

MCI (Montessori Centre International) (2009) *Literacy, Module 9*, Early Childhood Course. London: MCI.

MCI (2010) *Montessori Philosophy, Module 1*. London: MCI.

Miller, L. and Pound, L. (eds) (2011) *Theories and Approaches to Learning in the Early Years*. London: Sage.

Montanaro, S.Q. (1991) *Understanding the Human Being*. Mountain View, CA: Nienhuis Montessori USA.

Montessori, M. (1964) [1912] *The Montessori Method*. New York: Schocken Books.

Montessori, M. (1965) [1914] *Dr Montessori's Own Handbook*. New York: Schocken Books.

Montessori, M. (1966) [1936] *The Secret of Childhood*. Notre Dame, IN: Fides Publishers Ltd.

Montessori, M. (1989a) [1961] *What You Should Know About Your Child*. Oxford: ABC – Clio Ltd, Volume 4.*

Montessori, M. (1989b) [1946] *Education for New World*. Oxford: ABC – Clio Ltd, Volume 5.*

Montessori, M. (1989c) [1979] *The Child, Society and the World*. Oxford: ABC – Clio Ltd, Volume 7.*

Montessori, M. (1989d) [1975] *The Child in the Family*. Oxford: ABC – Clio Ltd, Volume 8.*

Montessori, M. (1991) [1918] *The Advanced Montessori Method – Volume 1*. Oxford: ABC – Clio Ltd, Volume 9.*

Montessori, M. (1992) [1949] *Education and Peace*. Oxford: ABC – Clio Ltd, Volume 10.*

Montessori, M. (1997a) [1976] *Basic Ideas of Montessori's Educational Theory*. Oxford: ABC – Clio Ltd, Volume 14.*

Montessori, M. (1997b) *California Lectures of Maria, 1915*. Oxford: ABC – Clio Ltd, Volume 15.*

Montessori, M. (2007a) [1949] *The Absorbent Mind*. Amsterdam: Montessori-Pierson Publishing Company, Volume 1.

Montessori, M. (2007b) [1912] *The Discovery of the Child* (originally published as *The Montessori Method*). Amsterdam: Montessori-Pierson Publishing Company, Volume 2.

Montessori, M. (2007c) [1955] *The Formation of Man*. Amsterdam: Montessori-Pierson Publishing Company, Volume 3.

Montessori, M. (2007d) [1948] *To Educate the Human Potential*. Amsterdam: Montessori-Pierson Publishing Company, Volume 6.

Montessori, M. (2007e) [1948] *From Childhood and Adolescence*. Amsterdam: Montessori-Pierson Publishing Company, Volume 12.

Montessori, M. (2007f) [1916] *The Advanced Montessori Method – Volume 2*. Amsterdam: Montessori-Pierson Publishing Company, Volume 13.

Montessori, M. (2012) *The 1946 London Lectures*. Amsterdam: Montessori-Pierson Publishing Company, Volume 17.

Montessori, M. (2013) *The 1913 Rome Lectures First International Training Course*. Amsterdam: Montessori-Pierson Publishing Company, Volume 18.

Montessori, M. Jnr (1992) [1976] *Education for Human Development*. Amsterdam: Montessori-Pierson Publishing Company, Volume 11.

Montessori St. Nicholas (2008) *The Guide To Early Years Foundation Stage in Montessori Settings*. London: MSN.

Montessori St. Nicholas (2011) *The Montessori St. Nicholas Charity Annual Review 2010*. London: MSN.

Morris, J.M. (1990) *The Morris-Montessori World List*. London: London Montessori Centre.

Morris-Coole, S. (2007) The control of error. *Montessori International*. October–December, issue 85, pp. 40–41.

Moyles, J. (ed.) (2005) *Excellence of Play*. Buckingham/Philadelphia, PA: Open University Press.

MSA (Montessori Schools Association) (2012) *Guide to the Early Years Foundation Stage in Montessori Settings*. London: Montessori St. Nicholas Charity.

NAMTA (North American Montessori Teachers' Association) (1987) *Montessori Under Three* (DVD). NAMTA.

NAMTA (1991) *Starting from Year Zero* (VHS). NAMTA.

NAMTA (2001) The Montessori adolescent: Analysis in retrospect. *The NAMTA Journal*, Volume 26, Number 3.

NAMTA (2006) Beyond school: Montessori in nature, home, teacher development and moral education. *The NAMTA Journal*, Volume 31, Number 2.

NAMTA (2007) The Montessori century concept: Continuing process in reality. *The NAMTA Journal*, Volume 32, Number 1.

NAMTA (2009) The first three years of life from all developmental perspectives. *The NAMPTA Journal*, Volume 34, Number 1.

Nutbrown, C. (2012) *Foundations for Quality: Independent Review of Early Education and Childcare Qualifications*. London: DfE. Online:

www.gov.uk/government/uploads/system/uploads/attachment_data/file/175463/Nutbrown-Review.pdf

Nutbrown, C., Clough, P. and Selbie, P. (2008) *Early Childhood Education, History, Philosophy and Experience*. London: Sage.

O'Donnell, M. (2014) *Maria Montessori: Critical Introduction to Key Themes and Debates*. London: Bloomsbury.

Piaget, J. (1963) *The Psychology Intelligence*. Totowa, JJ: Helicon Press.

Rambush, N. McC. (1962) *Learning How To Learn*. Baltimore: Helicon Press.

Read, H. (1943) *Education Through Art*. London: Penguin Books.

Rich, D., Casanova, D., Dixon, A., Drumond, M.J., Durrant, A. and Myer, C. (2005) *First Hand Experience: What Matters to Children: An Alphabet of Learning from the Real World*. London: Rich Learning Opportunities.

Robinson, M. (2003) *From Birth to One, The Year of Opportunity*. Maidenhead: Oxford University Press.

Siraj-Blatchford, J. and Brock, L. (2016) *Putting the Schema Back into Schema Theory and Practice: An Introduction to Schema Play*. Poole: SchemaPlay Publications. Online: www.schemaplay.com/Publications.html

Standing, E.M. (1984) *Maria Montessori, Her Life and Work*. New York: Plume.

Stoll-Lillard, A. (2004) *The Science Behind the Genius*. New York: Oxford University Press.

Stoll-Lillard, A. (2008) *Montessori: The Science of Genius*. New York: Oxford University Press.

Sylva, K., Melhuish, E., Sammons, P., Siraj-Blatchford, I. and Taggart, B. (2004) *The Effective Provision of Preschool Education (EPPE) Project: Findings from Pre-school to End of Key Stage 1*. Nottingham: Department for Education and Skills.

Vygotsky, L. (1978) *Mind in Society*. Cambridge, MA: Harvard University Press.

Wolf, A.D. (1996) *Nurturing the Spirit in Non-Sectarian Classrooms*. Hollidaysburg, PA: Parent Child Press.

Wolf, A.D. (2017) *Montessori for a Better World*. USA: Parent Child Press, division of Montessori Services.com.

Note: Please note that all the titles identified with * are now available from Montessori Pierson Publishing, Amsterdam.

Index

Page numbers in *italics* indicate an illustration